BY ANDREW HUSSIE

BOOK 2

PART 1
___

ACT 3
&
INTERMISSION

Act 3
"Insane Corkscrew Haymakers"

🧊 55　🧊 44　💧 66

Intermission
"Don't Bleed on the Suits"

🏃 14　🕐 1000　⬤ 1

ACT 3
INSANE CORKSCREW HAYMAKERS

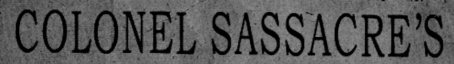

COLONEL SASSACRE'S
DAUNTING TEXT
MAGICAL FRIVOLITY OF AND PRACTICAL JAPERY

The Colonel amuses men marginally less soused than he on a sweltering Missisipi evening. In true Sassacre form he puts his astonishing julep intake to use with a textbook execution of "Butterfingers Solitaire."

The fancy border around every page of *Sassacre's Daunting Text* was affectionately borrowed from a copy of *Wizardology*, which I augmented with scribbles of naked people and dragons having sex with cars, and then gave to a friend. I put a picture of my face on the back cover, labeled "YOU'RE WELCOME," which she immediately tore off, because she thought it was weird. I guess it was a little weird, in a handsome kind of way.

Dear John,

You are no doubt reading this as a handsome and strapping young man! Why, the mangrit needed to lift the book is itself a sign of your maturity, not even to speak of the wisdom needed to grasp the nuance of <u>Sassacre's</u> time-tested mischief. I am so proud of you, grandson!

How I wish I could have delivered this heirloom to you in the flesh. But I am afraid it wasn't in the cards! For you see, John, like you, this book must yet take a journey! Its journey will end on the <u>Final Day</u> of my life, and even then will continue some. Though I suppose that will be up to your father. Perhaps he will discuss it with you one day, when he and you are ready.

> Dear John,

You are no doubt reading this as a handsome and strapping young man! Why, the mangrit needed to lift the book is itself a sign of your maturity, not even to speak of the wisdom needed to grasp the nuance of <u>Sassacre</u>'s time-tested mischief. I am so proud of you, grandson!

How I wish I could have delivered this heirloom to you in the flesh. But I am afraid it wasn't in the cards! For you see, John, like you, this book must yet take a journey! Its journey will end on the <u>Final Day</u> of my life, and even then will continue some. Though I suppose that will be up to your <u>Father</u>. Perhaps he will discuss it with you one day, when he and you are ready.

But it is your journey I am writing about to wish you luck! There will come a day when you will be thrust into another world. And once you arrive, that is only the beginning! You will soon delve even deeper into a realm of <u>Warring Royalty</u> in a <u>Timeless Expanse</u>. A realm of <u>Agents</u> and <u>Exiles</u> and <u>Consorts</u> and <u>Kernelsprites</u>. Of toiling <u>Underlings</u> and slumbering <u>Denizens</u>. A realm where four will gather, the <u>Heir of Breath</u> and <u>Seer of Light</u>, the <u>Knight of Time</u> and <u>Witch of Space</u>, and together they will <u>Ascend</u>.

John, if only you knew how important you were! I regret my passing came so early in your life. And yet I feel in my heart we have already met. But what I know for sure is that we will meet again!

Until then, John, I do hope your <u>Father</u> keeps you well fed!

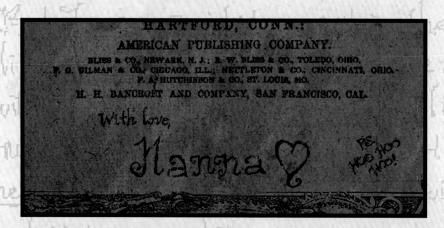

HARTFORD, CONN.:
AMERICAN PUBLISHING COMPANY.
BLISS & CO., NEWARK, N.J.; R. W. BLISS & CO., TOLEDO, OHIO.
F. G. GILMAN & CO., CHICAGO, ILL.; NETTLETON & CO., CINCINNATI, OHIO.
F. A. HUTCHINSON & CO., ST. LOUIS, MO.
H. H. BANCROFT AND COMPANY, SAN FRANCISCO, CAL.

With love,
Nanna ♡

P.S.
HOO HOO
HOO!

6   When you find out when she actually wrote this inscription, you will realize what a sly old prankster Jane is. Also, check out all those <u>Capitalized Underlined Terms</u>. Man, did I ever stop doing THAT as the story went along. See: Conceit_Abandonment on Wikipedia. (That article doesn't exist.)

A silly girl naps by her flowers. It is quite likely that she tired herself out with a variety of silly antics, as silly girls are often known to do. She may have a silly name too. Or maybe not. It is hard to say for sure without asking her.

But since she's slumbering peacefully, it would be a shame to wake her up. You might as well just give her a name right now.

> Enter name.

Through a variety of cunning characterization devices, we begin to develop a sense that this girl may be rather silly. In my creative writing workshops, I often suggest that in order to convey a character has a certain quality, use a word to describe the character repeatedly in their introduction.

7

Uh...

I guess...

I guess her name is Farmstink.

> Wake up!

I wonder which troll named her Farmstink? Do trolls even have farms? Maybe they call them musclebeast pastures.

You try to roust Farmstink from her slumber, but she is really down for the count!

It looks like she is holding some sort of NOTE.

> Retrieve arms from...

THEY'RE RIGHT THERE.

IN PLAIN SIGHT.

LOOK, THEY ARE FLASHING RED.

> Drop pumpkin on Farmstink.

What pumpkin?

You see no pumpkin, and frankly it is hard to imagine there ever was a pumpkin, in plain sight or otherwise.

Anyway, that would be a really terrible thing to do to poor, sweet Farmstink.

> Read note.

OKAY, THEY ARE NOT ACTUALLY FLASHING RED. THEY ARE JUST SORT OF BEING RED, BUT WHATEVER.

> Try again.

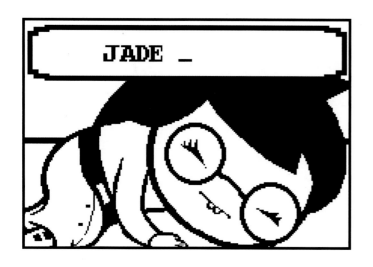

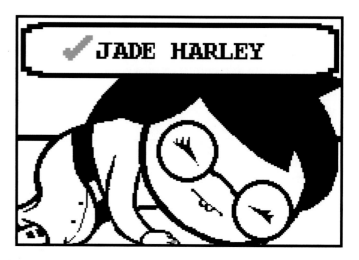

Look at Jade's lovely handwriting. I wish my handwriting was like that, or that I was even hypothetically capable of writing like that.

> Examine room.

Jade: Find something to support your garden planters with other than a thousand flower pots.

Your name is JADE. You have just woken from a restful nap, and as usual, you have no recollection of having fallen asleep. You have quite a number of INTERESTS. So many in fact, you have trouble keeping track of them all, even with an assortment of COLORFUL REMINDERS on your fingers to help you sort out everything on your mind. Nevertheless, when you spend time in your GARDEN ATRIUM, the only thing on your mind is your deep passion for HORTICULTURE.

What will you do?

>[S] Jade: Play a silly flute refrain.

We don't get her formal introduction until she journeys up to her room. This silly character is already BREAKING THE RULES. How is that possible? Can she even DO that? Jade, *Homestuck* has rules. Please try to respect them.

On this interactive page you get to play Jade's flute by hitting keys on the keyboard. All of the keys play a different terrible note. I used samples from my friend Jan, who recorded himself playing terribly. We originally used those clips in an edit of *Star Trek: TNG*, wherein Captain Picard played his flute very poorly while the Enterprise was under attack by the Borg. This might be the only thing that Jade and Picard have in common at all.

Wow, you really suck at this thing!

Maybe you should try playing an instrument you actually know how to play instead, like the one in your bedroom. Honestly you have no idea where this flute even came from. Things seem to appear and disappear around here all the time. Especially, to your unending chagrin, any sort of large orange gourd that might be lying around.

You consider throwing the flute down in disgust.

> Jade: Captchalogue flute.

On second thought, it was a perfectly nice flute and there is no reason to take your frustration out on it. You just need some practice.

But before you captchalogue the FLUTE you will need to set your FETCH MODUS first!

> Jade: Set modus.

I guess the implication here is that the flute appearified there from an exile station? But that doesn't make much sense. We never saw any flutes on those stations. Obscure theory: alt-universe Jade as an old woman sent this flute to her, because she always regretted not taking up the instrument as a young girl. Whew. Plot hole count: back down to zero.

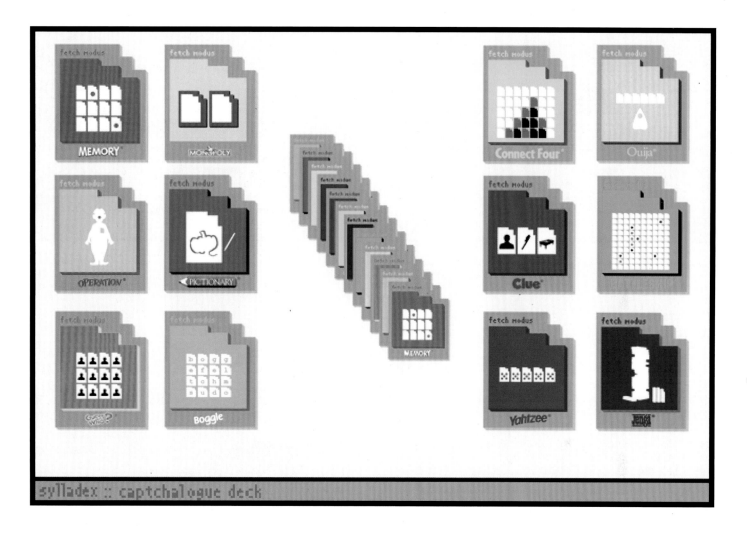

You have a wide variety of FETCH MODI to choose from. You were really excited when your GRANDPA bought you this MODUS SET for Christmas. He is a total badass, even if a little strict.

You typically opt for the MEMORY MODUS when it comes to matters of day-to-day practicality.

> Jade: Select Memory.

15

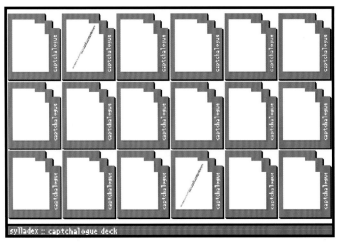

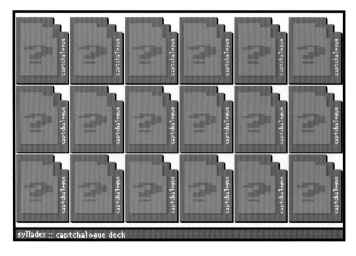

You set your modus to MEMORY, and captchalogue the FLUTE. You allot 9 cards to the modus from your deck, since that will be more than enough for your needs at the moment. The modus grabs 9 more cards for matching purposes.

The FLUTE is split up on two blank cards, and mixed randomly into the grid. To retrieve the item you must first pick one card, and then pick its matching card.

For the typical sylladexer this modus presents a frustrating guessing game and a lot of wasted time on mismatching. But you like it because you seem to have a knack for always guessing right on the first try!

> Jade: Squeal like a piglet and fertilize some plants.

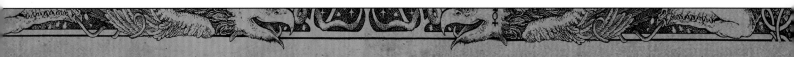

It is an awfully silly idea and is
basically a waste of everyone's
time. You will predictably disregard
this thought and focus on more
sensible objectives at once.

oh my god this is so much fun

Another pattern broken. She is supposed to reject the standard suggestion in the form of _____ like a _____ and _____ on your _____, just like John and Rose and Dave
did. She is not supposed to actually do it, let alone enjoy it. All this pattern breaking is starting to become a pattern. (Don't worry, she'll break that one too.)

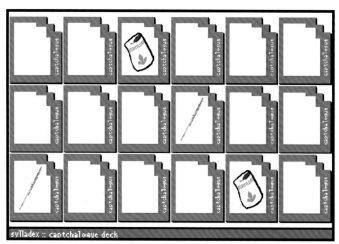
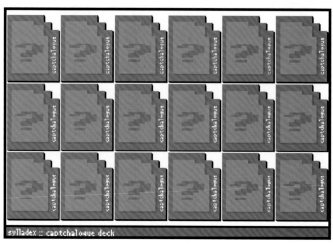

You captchalogue the BAG OF FERTILIZER.

> Jade: Consult colourful reminders.

You know what? I think I'm going to ditch the fancy border on the footer graphic for the rest of the book. Good grief, is this thing frivolous. It doesn't feel like I'm commenting on the book so much as it feels like I'm casting a spell.

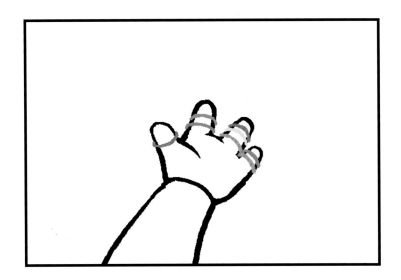

You tend to have a lot of things on your mind at once, and you can be a little forgetful. So you keep a variety of COLORED STRINGS on your fingers as reminders. Each one means there is something different to remember at a certain time.

In fact, looking at your index finger reminds you that there is something important to remember now! It is your friend John's birthday. The green string reminds you that John's birthday package will arrive today. The blue string ALSO reminds you that John's birthday package will arrive today, though in a way that means something slightly different.

You are further reminded that you have some things to do outside your house soon. But you should stop by your room first for some supplies, and most importantly, to see if John is online and wish him a happy birthday!

> Jade: Captchalogue the pumpkin growing next to you.

You snap up that PUMPKIN which seems suitably ripe for the taking. Hopefully the safety of your sylladex will prevent it from being spirited away like so many of its ephemeral predecessors.

> Jade: Exit this room.

There, that's better.

FYI, the green one on her pinky is reminding her to watch *Shrek 2* later.

You make your way to the middle of the GARDEN ATRIUM, where a stairwell joins the four ATRIUM WINGS.

Upstairs is your grandfather's LABORATORY as well as your BEDROOM.

> Jade: Captchalogue something.

Your MEMORY modus is hardly any fun without much stuff in it, so you decide to stock up on fresh produce to fill some more cards.

You pick a juicy red CRAB APPLE.

You go pick a nice looking KEY LIME.

Then a delicious MANDARIN ORANGE.
Those are your favorite.

And finally a ripe yellow EUREKA LEMON.

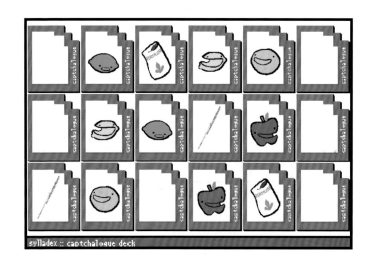

Modus fun aside, you feel it is impossible to have
too many fresh fruits and vegetables on hand.

> Jade: Go upstairs to bedroom.

These happy fruits appear throughout the rest of the story at some very odd times. I didn't remember until now that they all had special names. These names are never used again. What a shame.

You almost never use the stairs.

You TRANSPORTALIZE upstairs. Just above is your room.

> Jade: Ascend.

You enter your bedroom. On this side of the room you are immediately confronted with numerous artifacts highlighting your various INTERESTS.

"Ascend" is a loaded word in *Homestuck*, and it often portends some hella major shit going down. (Or up!!!) But ascending can also be no biggie. Like, hey, she just walked up the stairs and now she's in her room.

You are an avid follower of CARTOON SHOWS OF CONSIDERABLE NOSTALGIC APPEAL. You have a profound zeal for marvelous and fantastical FAUNA OF AN ANTHROPOMORPHOLOGICAL PERSUASION. You have an uncanny knack for NUCLEAR PHYSICS, and not infrequently can be found dabbling in RATHER ADVANCED GADGETRY. You enjoy sporadic fits of NARCOLEPSY; your love of GARDENING transcends the glass confines of your ATRIUM; and you are at times prone to patterns of PRECOGNITIVE PROGNOSTICATION.

You consider very briefly the question: What will you do?

But you quickly realize this is only one half of your room, and is therefore host to only half of your INTERESTS to choose from.

> Jade: Explore the other half of your room!

Over here there are yet more articles of your aforementioned INTERESTS, and then some.

Additional telltale signs of your enthusiasm for NOSTALGIC TELEVISION mingle with your assortment of GAME HUNTING FIREARMS. You are a SKILLED MARKSWOMAN, though your cross-hairs would never settle on an innocent creature, ANTHROPOMORPHICALLY PERSUADED OR OTHERWISE.

Your worktable is littered with equipment to facilitate your tinkering. For you, experimentation is not a particularly exact science, and you lean heavily on SHARP INTUITION for consistently and eerily optimal results. Nevertheless, you have still not been able to get that broad, flat gizmo there to work, which is a design you have borrowed from one of your GRANDPA'S more mysterious inventions.

You are a great admirer of his, and you are not alone. Your grandfather is a WORLD RENOWNED EXPLORER-NATURALIST-TREASURE HUNTER-ARCHEOLOGIST-SCIENTIST-ADVENTURER-BIG GAME HUNTER-BILLIONAIRE EXTRAORDINAIRE. He has taught you everything you know.

But in spite of all his lessons, it is still difficult to escape his stern lectures when you are on the way out of the house to run your errands. He spends most of his time in the GRAND FOYER, stewing in his own intensity and charisma.

And today will likely be no exception. Among the errands you have planned is to venture out to find your pet and best friend named BECQUEREL. This animal must be fed and he will not be happy if he is not. And if he is not happy then you will not be happy.

But first you really should dig out your COMPUTER and say hi to John!

NOW...

What will you do?

> Jade: Quickly retrieve firearms from wall.

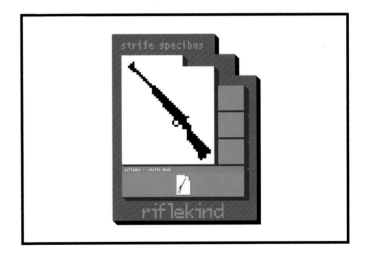

You equip your trusty HUNTING RIFLE. There would be hell to pay if grandad caught you leaving the house without it.

> Jade: Wonder why the design on your shirt changed.

Are you familiar with Humanimals? If you aren't, then shame on you. I will not explain Humanimals to you. Not here. Maybe in private, like in a dark alley, or on a foggy night down by the docks. If you are familiar with Humanimals, then here's what I have to say: Manthro Chaps are to Humanimals as Squiddles are to horrorterrors. Now you know the secret. /shhhhhh

There isn't much to wonder, really. You left the
WARDROBIFIER on its randomization setting.

You may contemplate which shirt design you favor the
most and commit to that setting in the near future.

> Jade: Captchalogue nearest Squiddles doll
and hug it.

Just before you can grab one, the powerful
ELECTROMAGNETS concealed in their underbellies
become activated, and two of them get all
tangled up with each other playfully.

You captchalogue the TANGLE BUDDIES.

> Jade: Lose interest in fauna and never
speak of it again.

Re: her posters, the "Green Slime Ghost" one I made not long into *Homestuck*'s run and sold it as one of the first prints. Which was a pretty esoteric product, now that I think about it. It portrays a fairly authentic-looking Japanese knockoff product based on Slimer from *Ghostbusters*, featuring Engrish and also "reverse Engrish" (i.e., phrases in Japanese which make very little sense to Japanese people). Also notice her *SBaHJ* furry poster, which was clearly a very thoughtful gift from Dave.

Oh, but you could NEVER do that.

What marvelous creatures they are. What a daring dream, to combine the finest qualities of humanity with the elegance and nobility of the animal kingdom. How you wish you could know their world. To hear one night those muted pawpads traipse up your stairs. A low but friendly growl unsettles your slumber, and as the sopor seeps from your eyes they detect a sharp pair of ears cutting moonlight. A mysterious wolven tongue invites. Wouldn't these ears suit you? Would not this proud long snout assist you in the hunt?

No need to answer. Words slough from the busy mind like a useless dead membrane as a more visceral sapience takes over. Something simpler is in charge now, a force untouched by the concerns and burdens of the upright, that farcical yoke the bipedal tow. It now drives you through the midnight brush, your paws whisking through creepers, unearthing with each bold stomp bright odors demanding investigation. But not for long, as you and your new friend must claim the night with piercing howls moonward.

You eat a weird bug and don't even care.

> Jade: Pick up your toys!

The weird anime furry to the left: for some reason I drew over this (once NSFW) furry art so that it had a human nose instead of some sort of cute catgirl snout. Why did I do that?? That's just awful. Also... PREEMPTIVE CALLBACK ZONE: not only does this panel get reused thousands of pages later with a different character, but the furry prose also gets recycled later, as morse code, in a completely unrelated situation. *Homestuck* is actually kind of weird, guys.

Speaking of which, you pick up and admire one of your MANTHRO CHAPS. They are wonderful friends and are always cheerful and pleasant fellows.

Why dear Mr. Coxcomb, how ever will you be received at the BARNYARD GALA without the trappings of a proper gentleman?

Each MANTHRO CHAP comes with a number of accessories, including articles of FORMAL ATTIRE, a VACCINATION KIT, and a DISHWASHER-SAFE SLOP TROUGH.

> Jade: Organize all your dolls.

You gather all your dolls into a rather cozy looking pile.

> Jade: Change wardrobifier setting.

You deactivate the WARDROBIFIER'S randomization mode and set it to cycle through these three shirt designs. The decision was tough, but you think you came to the best possible conclusion.

> Jade: Look out window.

Due to the real hypodermic needles supplied with Coxcomb's VACCINATION KIT, Manthro Chaps have been banned from all first-world AND third-world nations. Luckily, Jade lives in neither type of nation, so she and Coxcomb may attend the barnyard gala unfettered.

It is another beautiful day in your neighborhood. It is peaceful and quiet as usual. A rather imposing VOLCANO looms over your house, which has been inactive for centuries.

Though dormant on the surface, the volcanic activity deep underground provides your house with a source of GEOTHERMAL POWER. You are not sure why your grandfather decided to draw from this source of energy when he had the UNLIMITED POWER OF THE ATOM at his disposal. But it has been this way for as long as you can remember.

You have chalked it up to your family's longstanding propensity for eclectic fursuits wait you mean pursuits.

> Jade: Retrieve fursuit from magic chest.

What is this nonsense about fursuits!!! You do not own a fursuit. You think ANTHROPOMORPHIC FAUNA are really cute and enchanting and all, but it has never occurred to you to dress as one. Sure, it is fun to imagine what it would be like to run wild with a pack of wolves, or purr and frolic with a litter of kittens, but dressing up as an animal just seems ridiculous. It would still just be a silly girl draped in a raggedy synthetic tufty piece of crap, and seriously who are you trying to kid with that sort of baloney!

Anyway it is not a MAGIC CHEST, it it your GADGET CHEST, which you have adapted for storing a number of USEFUL GIZMOS. It was once your ORACLE'S TRUNK, a gift from your grandfather of course, and still contains many silly FORTUNE TELLING KNICKKNACKS, all of which are completely bogus.

> Jade: Open chest.

This page helps us understand exactly what kind of furry Jade is. Which is the casual kind, as opposed to the TOTAL WEIRDOS who like to dress up as animals and yiff each other and stuff, thus completely ruining the story. No, the story will have to wait until Act 5 to be ruined by those kinds of weirdos.

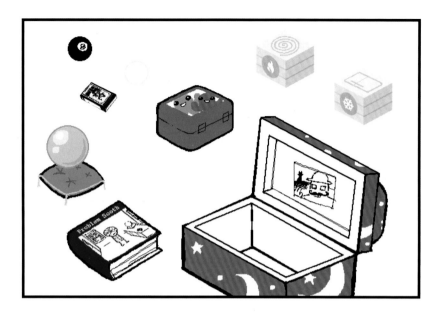

Among the FORTUNE TELLING KNICKKNACKS are these items: a CRYSTAL BALL plus compulsory VELVET PILLOW, a TAROT DECK, a MAGIC 8 BALL, a MAGIC CUE BALL, and one of your favorite books of all time, PROBLEM SOOTH.

Among the USEFUL GIZMOS are of course your COMPUTER, which you keep inside a FUN LUNCHBOX for easy transport, and a couple of gizmos you keep handy so you don't always have to make the long trip to the kitchen. There is a COOKALIZER for preparing delicious meals, and a REFRIGERATOR, a name which clearly is a wacky variation on the much more common household item, the REFRIGIFYIFICATOR.

> Jade: Examine magic 8-ball and magic cue ball.

These things are stupid and useless!

When the MAGIC 8 BALL isn't being frustratingly ambiguous, its forecast is always wrong! You have tested it numerous times with certain facts you know to be true. This is its reply when you ask if it is your friend John's birthday today. See? Stupid!

You guess maybe it could be used as a reverse-prediction device, and always trust the opposite of what it says. But that seems dumb to you. And anyway, the thing gives you a bad vibe. You might consider smashing it, but you are a little superstitious about whatever ominous consequences that might have, even if the occult talisman in question is a cheap piece of garbage.

Maybe Vriska started picking on Jade because she's all h8ing on magic 8-balls? Everyone knows 8-balls are GR8!!!!!!!! Come to think of it, this page is what retroactively led to Vriska's interest in 8-balls, her weird obsession with smashing them, and ultimately her entanglement with themes of luck, both good and bad. For all of this story's absurd and self-indulgent detours, it's pretty hard to find a totally useless page with no later relevance.

30

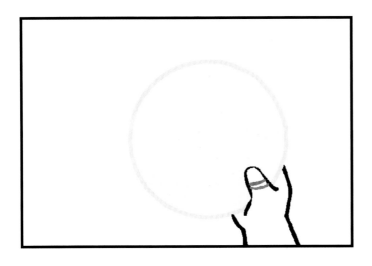

The MAGIC CUE BALL on the other hand is said to
make predictions with alarming precision and
specificity. Unfortunately it lacks a portal on its
surface that allows you to view the prediction.

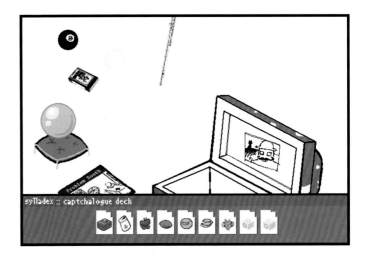

You put both of these pieces
of junk back in the box.

> Jade: Captchalogue refrigerator.

You take the REFRIGERATOR.

You might as well grab the COOKALIZER too.
No portable kitchen is complete without it.

You take your LUNCHTOP too, because obviously
you're going to be using that pretty soon.

Whoops, there goes your FLUTE. But who cares.

> Jade: Feed your friend.

That innocuous cue ball also has relevance later, in ways that are pretty seriously totally UNinnocuous. The only things in that chest that don't get brought up again are
the tarot deck, that pillow which could probably have been used to make a nice dress, and *Problem Sooth* (which you are dying to peek inside, I just know it). Also, the
fact that a picture of her grandpa is taped to the chest in the same place where John kept a photo of Harry Anderson maybe suggests that John views Anderson as a
grandfather figure. Or maybe Anderson WAS his grandpa?? Oh god, it's all adding up now...

Before you go out to feed BEC, you will need to prepare a meal for him.

You clear some space on your work table so you can set up your REFRIGERATOR and COOKALIZER.

Just for fun, Jade allows you to take a stab at matching the cards to use the gizmos. It doesn't present much of a challenge for her, so she figures she might as well step aside, while providing a few generous hints.

No, no... warmer. Warmer. Cooler. Cooler.

COLD.

Warmer...

Yes. NO. Cold. ICE COLD.

Warmer. Warmer...

Sometimes I think about how many thousands of pages I still have to put into books in order to finish this series, and I look at pages like this dedicated to playing a fake game of *Memory*, and I wonder to myself, "What am I doing with my life?"

32

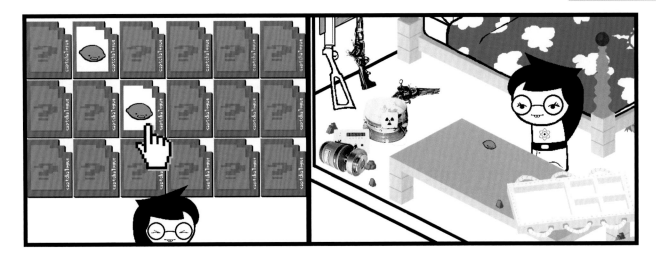

You have selected the KEY LIME.
Way to go.

> Try again.

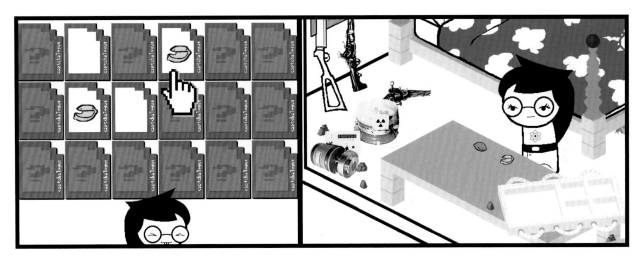

HOT. Wait...
No. Cold. Really cold. FROZEN FUCKING TUNDRA.

> Take another crack at this.

Now that I think about it, it probably wouldn't have been too much work to make this an actually playable game of *Memory*. Might have been a waste of time, though. What would be the bigger waste: the time it would take to do that, or the paper it took to print it in a book? What is the more valuable resource? Time or paper? I'm not sure they're comparable. Like comparing apples and oranges. And limes and lemons. Fruit jokes.

Congratulations, you advance your matching skill to the new level: YUKON HERO: LEGACY OF THE FROSTBITE AMPUTEE. Jade is beginning to regret breaking the fourth wall for this ill advised escapade.

> Ok, one more time.

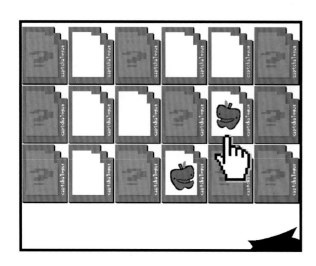 

If it were known in advance how terrible you were going to be at this matching game, the author may have given second thought to preparing this cool interactive Flash application.

Look at all these fruits on the loose. Good luck trying to settle them down.

And now on this page I'm lampooning the fact that this *wasn't* a Flash game. It was just a series of automated gifs that made it appear as if the "player" was a bumbling idiot. Anyway, some other things to say about this page: Jade regrets breaking the fourth wall here, but later she breaks a much bigger one. Also: fruits on the loose. "Fruits on the loose" is a funny phrase. That's all.

You just deploy the gadgets yourself.

> Jade: Stick fruits in the refrigerator to keep them fresh.

These fruits are unlikely to become less impudent any time soon regardless of where they are stored, but you stick them in anyway.

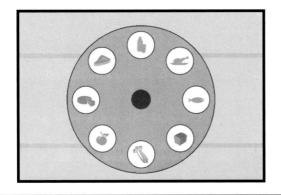

You take a look at the REFRIGERATOR'S rotary interface. You wonder what he is in the mood for today?

> Jade: Press the steak button.

Wait, it's a rotary interface, but it still has buttons? Oh, that's just a dumb reader command from someone who thinks they're buttons. I probably called that guy out on his mistake on the next page.

35

Ok, well it's a rotary dial so there are no buttons to press, but whatever that doesn't really matter.

You dial up a thick T-BONE STEAK, which you are sure Becquerel is in the mood for because he is in the mood for steak every day and is never in the mood for anything else.

But he does like his steak well cooked.

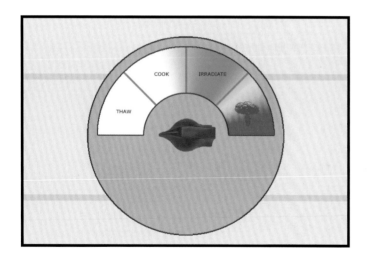

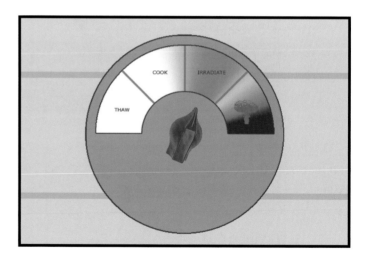

> Jade: Lightly irradiate steak.

He does prefer his steak rare after all.

But you will not dignify the thought of turning the knob much further because you are not retarded.

Yes, see? I pointed out that it was a rotary dial, not a radial arrangement of push-buttons. I go to the trouble of inventing a quirky interface for this food gizmo, and it's like pearls before swine. I then go on to say it doesn't really matter. I guess it doesn't. I don't know, the whole thing is ruined now. THE ROTARY FOOD DIAL THINGY IS RUINED FOREVER.

You captchalogue the IRRADIATED STEAK and save it for your trip outside.

You probably shouldn't waste much more time. You wouldn't want all those nice depleted steak isotopes to settle down.

> Jade: Examine the atomic bass by your bed.

You wouldn't exactly call it an atomic bass, but it is heavily customized to accommodate a high level of musical virtuosity, the perfect instrument for the eclectically spirited.

You've tuned the strings way down of course because your stumpy arms can't reach the low notes.

You switch your ECLECTIC BASS to its advanced setting.

But you promptly switch it back, since obviously it's too complicated to play it in person like this. The default setting is your preferred mode for casual jamming.

And since you can't possibly waste enough time playing music, casually jam is exactly what you're gonna do.

>[S] Jade: Play a hauntingly relaxing bassline.

> Jade: Captchalogue bass.

Here we confirm that Jade lives on that island we saw at the end of Act 2. Sometimes I feel these notes would benefit from an OBVIOUS TRIVIA ZONE, about stuff that should be obvious, but you never know. Her house is modeled after her moon tower on Prospit. The ruins are a model of the Incipisphere, with the frog in the center representing Skaia (which is where a giant frog is supposed to go). Prospit is in close orbit, and so is attached to the main temple (broken off). The four planets surround it in the Medium, which is represented by water. The circular edge of the crater is the Veil (consisting appropriately of meteors). And just outside is Derse (also broken). The volcano is called the Forge, which also plays a key role in the overall system here. Oh, and the ruins are seven levels tall, representing the seven gates one needs to ascend through to reach Skaia.

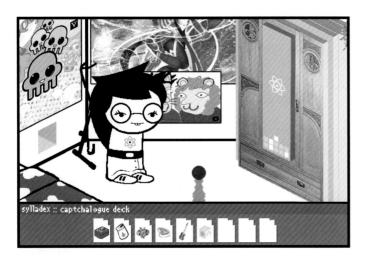

You take the PORTABLE AMP from the WALL SOCKET too.

> Jade: Open lunchtop.

You like to make yourself comfy in your plushy pile before getting down to business with your computer.

> Jade: Get down to business.

> Jade: Activate Pesterchum.

There is really a long and aggressively revisited tradition of people being in piles of things in *Homestuck*. I guess it started with Dave being in the puppet pile in the last act. Plushies, pillows, horns, robot parts, you name it. Okay, it might actually only be those four things? Anyway, you get the idea.

Hey look, John is online! Hooray!

Also it looks like Dave pestered you about something yesterday but you missed it.

> Jade: Pester John.

You greet John but he does not respond.
He is undoubtedly gallivanting around his
house in a state of barely restrained
birthday mirth. He may also be retrieving
the two packages and the two envelopes
which you are certain came in the mail
for him earlier.

You will wait a little while and see if
he returns before you head out.

> Jade: See if Dave left you a
sweet new rap.

It does not appear so, but you just never
know with that crazy and cool guy.

Sooooo coooooooool.

turntechGodhead [TG] **began pestering gardenGnostic** [GG] **at 2009-04-12 -- 23:14**

TG: hey
TG: oh
TG: youre asleep again arent you
TG: or do you even know if you are
TG: i still dont know how that works
TG: its like nothing means anything
TG: its so cool getting hella chumped by your coquettish damn riddles all the time
TG: i dont know why i believe anything you say im like the grand marshal of gross chumpage
TG: waving around my faggoty chumpductor baton
TG: assitant director of chumpography
TG: celebrated author ernest chumpingway
TG: wait weak
TG: chumpelstiltskin
TG: uh
TG: chumpeldipshit
TG: yeah
TG: youre asleep y/n?
TG: a/s/l?
TG: s = species
TG: baboon?
TG: kangaroo rat?
TG: if kangaroo rat yiff twice plz
TG: ok well youre not saying anything so i guess whether youre nonawake or unasleep or whatever youre just not around and im wasting good material
TG: even worse im wasting a killer fursona here
TG: like
TG: i dont know like a wide open v shaped leotard and a fuck ton of body paint
TG: some like sinewy back arching cirque du soleil looking motherfucker
TG: always low to the ground gettin a good prowl on
TG: like i dropped my keys in the dark
TG: nimblest son of a bitch who had the gumption to glue a nasty pair of latex cat lips to his face
TG: for a reason that wasnt a joke
TG: jade hey
TG: where are you
TG: seriously im sitting here tonight with a fucking bag of kibble jacked open on my lap and primed for goddamn bear
TG: and youre gone

Just another one of Dave's many, many conversations where he spends most of the time talking to nobody.

TG: btw my name is Akwete Purrmusk
TG: hardest buttock in the jungle
TG: tempered steel
TG: hey yeah just wanted to give you this remix i finished
TG: here
turntechGodhead [TG] sent **gardenGnostic [GG]** file "explore remix.mp3"
TG: so yeah
TG: you dont have to respond to any of that btw
TG: ill probably forget half the shit i said anyway
TG: talk to you tomorrow

You open the FRESHJAMZ MEDIA PLAYER and add Dave's remix to the playlist.

>[S] Jade: Open FreshJamz!

> Jade: Open Echidna and go to mspaintadventures.com

You open your web browser and visit MSPA.

You navigate to a random page in the middle of the latest epic.

Looks like he was just finishing up some sort of weird tangential intermission here. Whatever it was, it clearly advanced the plot in no relevant way whatsoever.

> END INTERMISSION.

With the (playable!) FRESHJAMZ playlist, we are provided with the implication that these are all songs produced by the kids collaboratively. Their icons indicate who was involved with the songs. Just another sign earlier in the story that these kids have some musical talent and this is the sort of thing they do with their spare time. This is one of those things that starts getting buried as we move along. For instance, we never quite get to see God Tier Jade picking up the old bass and rocking out. Which is a shame.

> |
> [S] MIDNIGHT CREW: ACT 1031
>

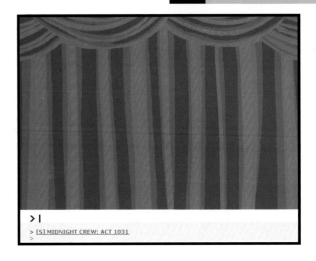

> |
> [S] MIDNIGHT CREW: ACT 1031
>

>[S] MIDNIGHT CREW: ACT 1031

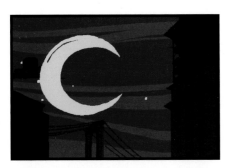

As we already know, the in-story MSPA.com is host to a long *Midnight Crew* adventure instead of *Homestuck*, the reverse of the case in our universe. But it DOES have a *Homestuck* intermission, whereas in our universe, *Homestuck* has a *Midnight Crew* intermission—which takes place immediately after this act! /OBVIOUS TRIVIA ZONE

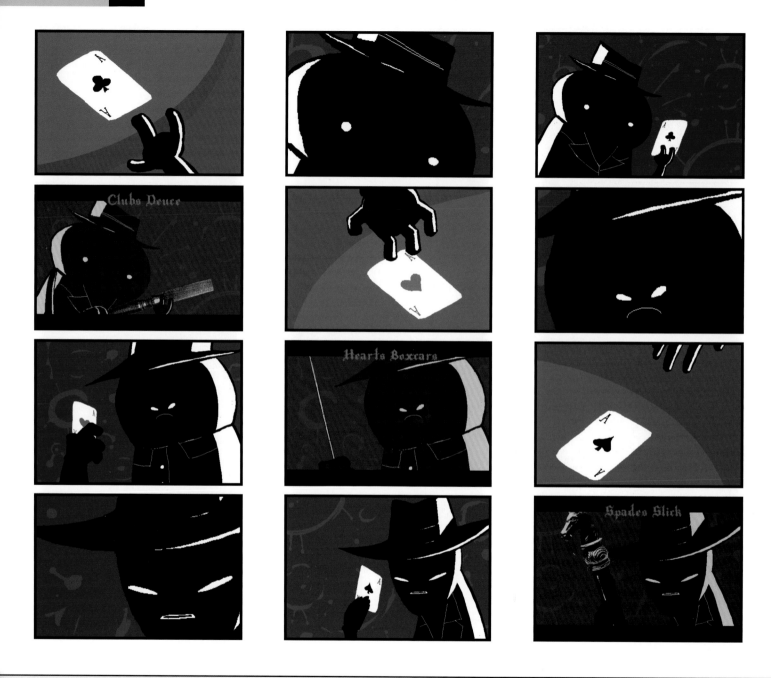

The Midnight Crew have item/weapon duality, just like in *Problem Sleuth,* which is the fictional realm they originated from. But it's almost a hybrid inventory system with an added dash of *Homestuck*, since the items that become weapons are always playing cards (you know, kinda like captchalogue cards). The four aces in the deck represent their primary weapons: the horse hitcher, the car antenna, the table leg, and the pool cue.

You've killed a little time,
but still no sign of John.

gardenGnostic [GG] began pestering
turntechGodhead [TG] at 2009-04-13 --
12:36

GG: hi dave!!
TG: hey sup
GG: not much sup with you!!
GG: bro! hehehe
TG: haha
TG: good one
TG: s'alright being chill i guess you
know how it goes
GG: great! feeling cool today?

> Jade: Pester Dave.

The Felt are the MC's adversaries in the actual *Homestuck* intermission. Fifteen members (plus their boss), each representing a billiard ball. They are all time travelers, and mostly a bunch of incompetent goons. The surface of a pool table is made of felt, hence the name of the gang. Also, I guess they are a little reminiscent of a bunch of green puppets, so there's that.

GG: mr cool guy?
TG: oh man you know it
GG: sooooo cooooooool!!!
TG: you know shit is ice cold up in here
TG: shit is wicked bananas i am telling you
GG: :D
GG: so have you talked to john today???
TG: yeah we were just talking a while ago about how he sucks at his sylladex
TG: can you believe he uses stack that kid is ridiculous
GG: lol
GG: well that doesnt sound like much fun!
TG: what was it you use again...
TG: wait nm
TG: i forgot whenever we talk about your goofy modusses i get a migraine. what do you want with john
GG: :)
GG: i want to tell him happy birthday and ask him about his birthday package!
TG: oh yeah
TG: i was being sort of cagey and told him to check the mail cause i was wondering if mine came yet
GG: i think it did!
TG: yeah?
GG: and i think mine came too
TG: so uh
TG: i guess you want to know if he likes it or something?
GG: no!!!!!!!
GG: he will not open it
GG: he will lose it!!!
TG: oh
TG: uh
TG: wow sorry to hear that i guess?
GG: no its good actually!
GG: because he will find it again later when he really needs it
GG: which of course is why i sent it in the first place!
TG: see like
TG: i never get how you know these things
GG: i dont know
GG: i just know that i know!
TG: hmm alright
GG: anyway i have to go!
GG: i have to feed bec which is always a bit of an undertaking

Hey, another copy/pasted conversation. We read this back in Act 2, before we knew a dang thing about Jade. Goofy moduses? What could those be? Ah yes, a bunch of board games. Really, it was so obvious in hindsight. She can tell the future? What's up with that? I guess we still don't know yet. She has a devilbeast? Well, whatever it is, we know it likes green steak. A grandad too? These are things we still need to learn. That's what a story is. A series of things you need to find out. First you learn about all the things you need to find out. And then you eventually find them out.

```
TG: man
TG: if i were you i would just take that fucking devilbeast out behind the woodshed and blow
its head off
GG: heheheh!
GG: i dont think i could if i tried!!!
TG: yeah
TG: say hi to your grand dad for me too ok
GG: ._.
GG: yes i guess an encounter with him is almost certain
GG: it is usually........
GG: intense!!!
TG: well yeah isnt it always with family
TG: but he sounds like a total badass
GG: yeah he totally is!!!
GG: anyway gotta go!
TG: see ya
GG: <3
```

>[S] Dave: STRIFE.

Dave commiserating with Jade about intense family encounters is a nice way to transition to the beginning of an intense encounter with his own family member. That is some really on-point transitioning there. Nice going, me.

In Round 1 of Dave's strife with Bro, he warms up against his old puppet sparring buddy, Lil Cal. Bro operates Cal while moving so fast you can't see him. It's suggested that this is a pretty common battle routine for the Strider brothers, an extreme training regimen to prepare Dave for battle. It's almost as if Bro is training him to face last boss. Or it would be, if last boss had the slightest thing to do with this creepy puppet, which of course is preposterous.

Cal easily outmaneuvers Dave, and the result is his comedic humiliation. But what would probably be even funnier is if it turned out that after a while, Bro stopped operating Cal, and Dave just continued to struggle with him, believing he was still being operated through flashstep puppetry. Bro just watches from the distance as Dave grapples with a limp puppet.

At the end of the animation, Cal dances on Dave's head for infinite minutes. Most of those infinite minutes have been omitted here for brevity.

Rose is online.

> Jade: Pester Rose.

TT: I require a font of frighteningly accurate yet infuriatingly nonspecific information.
TT: Do you know where I can find a wellspring of this sort?
GG: hahaha yes ok but we cant talk for long!!!
TT: You have plans?
GG: well yes i do but its just that you will lose your internet connection soon!!!!!
GG: and we wont talk again for a pretty long time
GG: not until you enter!
TT: Enter?
GG: yeah!
TT: This is what I was talking about.
TT: This was the itch that needed scratching.
TT: My avarice for the inscrutable. It is limitless.
GG: lol what did you want to know?
TT: You've been insisting today was the big day.
TT: We would all play a game you didn't know the name of.
TT: A game you said I'd get in the mail, and did.
TT: One that would help me answer some questions.

"TT: Enter?" Yes, Rose. Enter. It's the title of the animation at the end of this act.

TT: But Strider is being obtuse, I can't catch John at his computer, you don't even have the game yourself, and on top of all that, my internet is unstable.
TT: So are you sure today is the day?
GG: there sure are a lot of challenges but yes i am sure!!
GG: dave is cool, you know he will come around when the time is right
GG: he just has a lot of work to do first
GG: and so do you!
GG: youll need to keep searching for a stable signal and power source, it will be hard but dont give up!!!
GG: and dont worry about me either, focus on playing with john first
GG: it all starts with you two!
TT: Is there nothing else you can say to prepare me for this?
TT: I'm sure you think little of blithely upsetting dark forces with Grandpa Moreau over there on Hellmurder Island, but honestly I've only read a few books on it.
GG: haha dark? thats ridiculous!
GG: i dont really know what to tell you other than its not going to be what you think it is
GG: and most importantly you will have your questions answered, but they will be the ones you havent thought to ask yet!
GG: just be patient and be brave youll see
GG: it will be fun!!!!!!
GG: uh oh looks like youve got to go
GG: take care rose! <3<3<3

-- **tentacleTherapist** [TT] ceased pestering gardenGnostic [GG] at 12:54 --

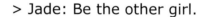

> Jade: Be the other girl.

You are now the other girl several hours in the future.

It appears a secret passage in the mausoleum has been opened.

It's getting awfully toasty in here. You gather up your belongings, including your dead cat.

> Rose: Descend.

When Jade says there are questions Rose hasn't thought to ask yet, she mainly means questions like, "Will I get totally hammered and make out with an alien?"

52

> Jade: Stop being the other girl and pester John again.

You've spent enough time for now concerning yourself with the future of your friends.

John will not be available until later. By then he will have his hands full, as will you.

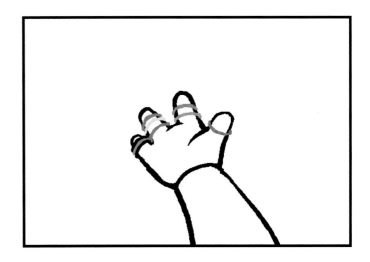

You pack up your LUNCHTOP and get ready to take care of some business downstairs.

>[S] Jade: Descend.

Try as you might, you can't stop your mind from drifting to the fate of your friends. You dwell on a particular configuration of REMINDERS on your finger.

That last panel is the intro frame to the battle animation on the next page. The particular configuration of reminders she's referring to is on her pinky, where two black strings sandwich a blue string. The blue one represents John, and the black ones represent the two ogres surrounding him. I guess she put those there so she could remind herself that at this point in the story, John is getting owned by a couple of ogres? That's definitely something she would want to remember, especially since she can't do anything about it, and doesn't do anything about it. But the point is, SHE REMEMBERED!

Behold, the mighty Pogo Hammer. Once John's dangerous childhood nemesis in the form of a backyard pogo ride. Now a similarly self-jeopardizing implement of only marginal combat value. Just think how easily one misfiring BOING could send him launching off the roof—or maybe just send the hammer careening back in his face?

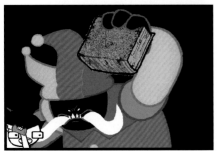

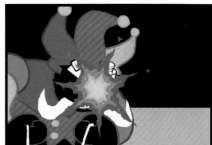

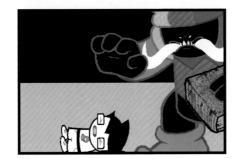

Consider how poignant it is that John spends this infinitely looping battle getting demolished by familiar items from his childhood. First getting clobbered by the huge heirloom joke book left to him by his grandma, and then getting lassoed by the old tire swing from his front yard, which surely brought him years of joy. How poignant is that? Way, way poignant.

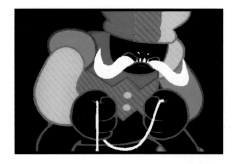
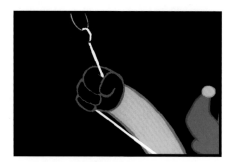
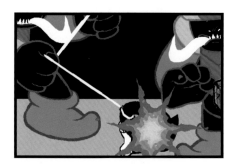

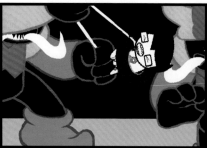

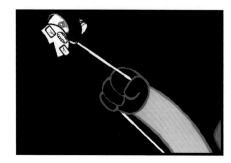

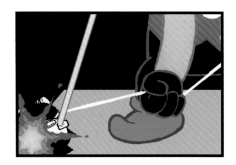

This maneuver is actually very similar to a move that someone does in an old *Street Fighter* game. I honestly don't remember if that's where I got the idea for it, though. I probably just asked myself, "How's a huge dude gonna take out some trash with a tire swing?" And correctly determined there was literally only one way it could be done.

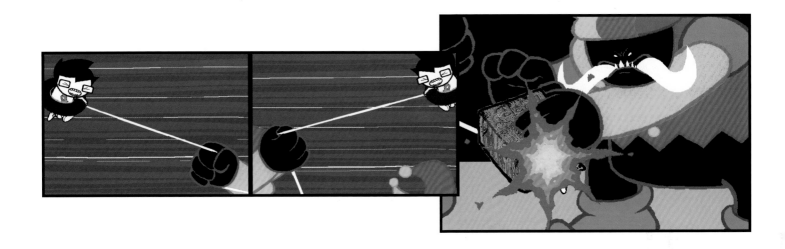

The Crude Ogres may be giant, bullying assholes, but you really have to admire their teamwork.

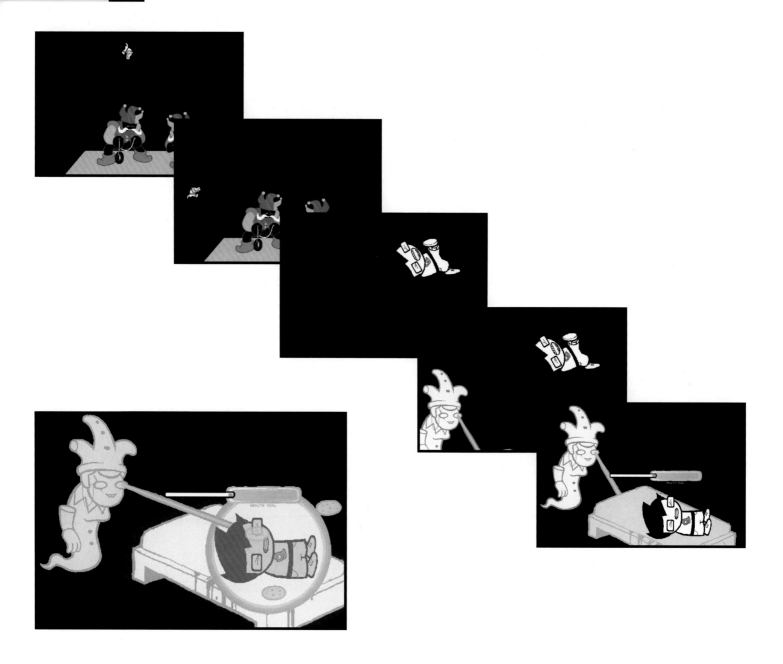

Nannasprite has healing powers, of course. It's unclear whether other sprites have these powers, as she's the only one who exhibits them. But then, it makes sense that she would have these abilities, since in a different world she is the Maid of Life. There you go, some more dots were just connected for you. You now understand nearly 1% of *Homestuck*.

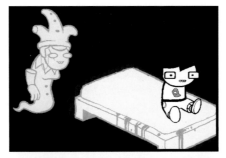

> Also in the future...

But years, not hours...

Under bare white branches a sentry wakens.

The battle then loops like that eternally, with John being dealt the same savage beating only to be revived by Nannasprite and sent back in for more abuse. His suffering is limited only by your willingness to watch it for hours, or failing that, leaving the page open in your browser and forgetting about it for days. :(

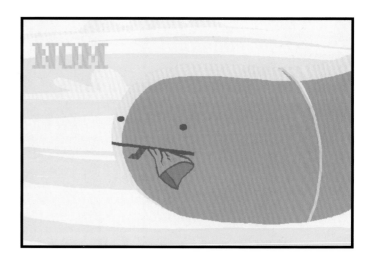

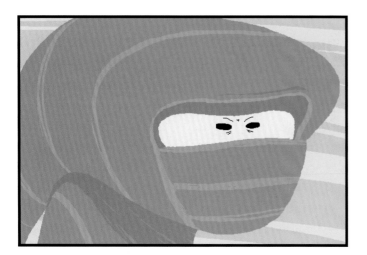

The robotic sentry worm was maybe going to be a friend to PM in the same way that Serenity is to WV. And it kind of was, for a while. But then she moved on. The main problem with the arrangement is that it's hard to become BFFs with a metal worm that's confined to its station. (Not to mention a station that blows up later.)

```
================================================================
[Z001] some stuff about captcha codes and punch card alchemy
================================================================
```

is anyone actually reading any of this?? or are they all
dead. i don't know if anyone besides us is even alive and
playing the game or if anybody even really cares what we
have to say!

rose said i should add some stuff to this faq if anything
occurred to me, so i guess i'm doing that. i figure at the
very least it will be a good reference for just us to use.
but dave probably won't read any of this because he's sort
of this whopping stupid horse butt. whatever.

i finally figured out what those weird codes on the back
of captchalogue cards are for. well maybe not what they're
ALWAYS for, but a way that sburb has exploited them for an
in-game purpose. every captcha'd item stamps the card with a
unique code, and a gizmo in sburb called the punch designix
will punch a unique pattern of holes in a card which is derived from that code. the punched card can then
be used with other gizmos to duplicate the item and/or combine it with another item.

i got to thinking about this and with my amazing hacker skillz i noticed a trend. the hole pattern is based
on a fairly simple cipher, converting the captcha code to binary and then the binary pattern is punched,
where 1 is a punched hole, and 0 is an unpunched slot.

so, umm... here's the table just to be clear.

0->0, 1->1, 2->2, 3->3, 4->4, 5->5, 6->6, 7->7, 8->8, 9->9

A->10, B->11, C->12, D->13, E->14, F->15, G->16, H->17, I->18, J->19, K->20, L->21, M->22, N->23, O->24
P->25, Q->26, R->27, S->28, T->29, U->30, V->31, W->32, X->33, Y->34, Z->35

a->36, b->37, c->38, d->39, e->40, f->41, g->42, h->43, i->44, j->45, k->46, l->47, m->48, n->49, o->50
p->51, q->52, r->53, s->54, t->55, u->56, v->57, w->58, x->59, y->60, z->61

?->62, !->63

there are a couple oddball characters ! and ? at the end to bring it up to 63 (0 thru 63 = 64 total, i.e.
6 bits). cause the binary representation of the captcha code chars are 6 bits each, which have a range of
0-63.

so for instance the captcha code for the hammer is "nZ7Un6BI". look up the index for 'n' first, which is
49. the binary of 49 is 110001. keep doing that for all the chars and you get:

n=110001 Z=100011 7=000111 U=011110 n=110001 6=000110 B=001011 I=010010

OK... that's the pattern that will be punched on the card, BUT...

John contributes to Rose's walkthrough. This is strictly for COMPSCI nerds. If you are not a COMPSCI nerd, skip this page immediately, or write me a short angry
note here: _____

the bits are arranged top to bottom, left to right, in four columns, like this:

```
1010
1010
0001
0100
0101
1111
1000
0101
0100
0110
1111
1000
```

or punched on a card, like this:

```
r#A&G&AAAAAAAAAAAAAAAAAAAAAAAA&&GGGGGGGh@@
;H9XXh&AAAAAAAAAAAAAAAAAAAAAAh3XXXXXXX2@@
;H3XX                 AhXXXXXX22@M,.:;;;,
;H33h                 @@GG&&&Gh9hA#@@@@@@
;H39A                 ;:.,,,,,,,,XA&AAA&@@
;H3hH                 5#333X2@@
;H3hH  r;;;;s,    ;r;::;,    2@X2X25@@
;H3hH  ;;:::r,    :r::::;    X#X2X253AH####@B
;H3hH  ;:.,,,r.    :;,,,;:   X#XXX22XGHBMMM#@r
;H3hH  ;;::;r,    ;;::;;     h@&hhXX39hh99&@;
;H3hH              :i;;;rr   r9ss5hXX999329@:
;H3hH              :r::::;;   .@3X3;.:SX3@:
;H3hH       rr;;;s;          :@hX9r.;3X3@:
;H3hH       .;;::;,          :@9X9rs.533@:
;H3hH       ;;,,,,;:    ;i;;;rs   :@9XG::r9X3@:
;H3hH       :,,,;,    ;::::;:   :@9Xh;..::X9@:
;H3hH  ir;;;i..;,,,r,:i;;;s:.r,,,;:  :@9XG3,i3X3@:
;H3hH  :::::;.:;,,;..;:::;;. ;,,,;:  :@99&i:r9X3@:
;H3hH  r;:,,r,               :@Gr;srs3X3@:
;H3hH  :,,,,;.               :@A.,XS5923@:
;H3hH       ss;;;i,    ;5;;;si   :@G&Ar, 2X3@:
;H3hH       ,;::::;.    ,;,,,;::  :@Gh&i; XX3@:
;H3hH       ;;,,,r:          :@Gii;.,3X3@:
;H3hH       ,:,,,;,          :@hir,X;2X3@:
;H3hH       ;;,,,r,;i;;;sr       :@hhAsi;2X3@:
;H3hH       .:,,,: ::::::.       :@h9XrisXX3@:
;H3hH  5r;;;5,;;:::r,,r:::r::2rrriS   :@h3i ;5923@:
;H3hH  ,::::;  ,...., ,....,. :,,,,,  :@93&srrXX3@:
;H3hH  s;:::s,               :@93G,;.;39@:
;H3hH  .....,               :@9XGs. X33@:
;H3hH                       :@9Xh;9,XX3@:
;H3hH                       ,@93G,5;SX3@:
;H3hH9AHHHHHHHHHHHHHHHHHHHHHHHHHHHHHHHHHA3hM93hhs2923@:
;H99&B#@@@@@@@@############################B&XXX3hGhX23@:
;H939hSsS&:s&h99999999999999999999999993XX2XXXXXX22X@:
;H3X23r ;G. hX22222222222222222222222222222222222252@:
:@#MM#AAG#Ah#MBBBBBBBBBBBBBBBBBBBBBBBBBMMMMMMMMMBHM@:
 ;MHHB###M##HHHHHHHHHHHHHHHHHHHHHHHHHHHHHHHHHHHHAAA#,
```

wow ok that pretty much looks like shit, but you get the idea.

so to combine two items you just overlap two punched cards. only the places where both cards have a hole will show through, so it's sort of like a bitwise AND operation on both cards. the new pattern gives you the code for the new item.

for instance combining the code for a hammer (nZ7Un6BI) and a pogo ride (DQMmJLeK) gives a new code with less holes obviously, which translates to 126GH48G. that hole pattern went on to make the pogo hammer, which is so rad you have no idea. i've also wondered if you can combine items in other ways, like a bitwise OR. that means combining the cards to get MORE holes, not less, i.e. the new pattern has a hole for every hole on either card. this pattern would be accomplished by DOUBLE PUNCHING A CARD!! like, two codes, one card. i've got to try that some time.

but there are some mysterious things about all this. first of all, with all the hole slots there are 48 bits in total, which means there are almost 300 trillion possible codes. and 300 trillion sounds huge! but when you consider it is supposed to account for ALL CONCEIVABLE ITEMS, including all the wacky combinations of stuff, it suddenly doesn't seem that big!

this leads me to believe that not every combination of item has a viable duplicate. but this is kinda obvious anyway, since there are many combinations of punch cards that will produce either a blank card (with AND) or a totally punched card (with OR). so there are lots of dud combinations out there, and many that will just lead to the same pattern. like for instance a gun and an atom bomb could make some sort of ULTIMATE DEATH RAY, but for that matter a shoe horn and a potted plant could lead to the exact same pattern!!!!! so weird.

also it seems like combined items will always have patterns with either much fewer holes or much more holes than more "ordinary" items, which will occupy the vast meaty middle of all possible patterns. it is strange and counter intuitive that more complex objects have simpler patterns but hey, there you have it.

I like the implication that not only did John take the time out of his quest to type this, but he also apparently downloaded some sort of ASCII art generator to make the hideous captchalogue card and ghost. That's some dedication. It's a shame, because I'm pretty sure even Rose got sick of maintaining this guide not long after this entry.

but all this sorta makes me guess this system can be cracked in some way. like if you have a complicated item and you want to "extract" simpler item components from it, there might be some algorithm for deriving the pattern you want, or at least narrowing down the possibilities. there might also be ways of charting through the simpler patterns on both ends of the bit spectrum, and pinning down the ones that will make cooler stuff. who knows.

i want to ask jade about this because she's really good at this sort of thing somehow even though she doesn't have my leet haxxor cred. too bad she makes herself so scarce all the time. jade if you ever read this let me know what you think!

```
                 ;AHHHHHHHHHHBr
                @@@@@@@@@@@@@@B
            h@&5s.,,,,,,,,,,r#@3
           @@@...:::::::::::::,@@@
          ;@A .,,:;;;;;;;:,::;@@@
         @@#r,BBA;;;;;;;AMM;:, 9@
        :H@@2 .;@@M:;;;;;:B@@;::.r#A:
        @@@2:..::,..,:::::::,...,;::,,@@#
        @@: ..;;;@@@@@@@@@@@@;;;;::r@@
        @G ,;;:#@            i@r,;;;:.&@
        @#.:;;,@@            ,@r,;;;:.9@
        &Ah,,;,@@;           ,@r:;;;5@@
         x@@i,,s#@s         XA&;:;;:,@@@&:
        .i@M.,.:@@9       h##@2.:;;;X@XS&@A
         @B.,,:i@@@@@@@@h,,:;;;:rX  .5@@
          @@@;,..:s2x25r:.,,:::;:,,,::,@@
          s@@#;...... ..,s5XXi;;;;;;:2@&;;.
          B@@hhGGGGGAA&@@@H:;;;;;;:,r@@@@@@r
          5@###@@@@@@#Hi..,;;;;;;;;;:,,,.@@@.
          A@     ...... ..::;;;;;;;;:,,,. @@;
           ,@5..,,:::::::;;;;;;;;;;;@A::#@@@@
           @@@r;:,,:::::::::::rM@@@@@@@
           2@@@@SXXXXXXXXXX2x@@@
             X@@@@@@@@@@@@@@
```

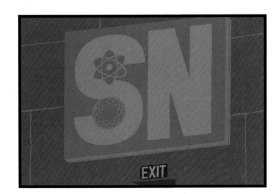

John's talking about hacking codes to theoretically extract simpler items. Which is exactly what he does later to make the rocket pack. So there you go. This entry was not merely a nerdish indulgence but also provided critical foreshadowing, which you skimmed over.

You enter the LABORATORY.

> Rose: Look for mad scientists.

There are no scientists to be found,
mad or otherwise. Or anyone for that matter.
The lab appears to be deserted.

There is a KIOSK though.

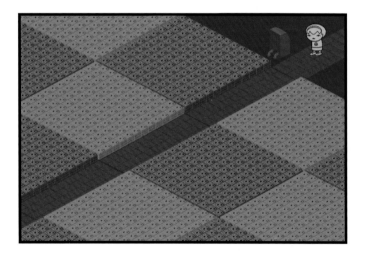

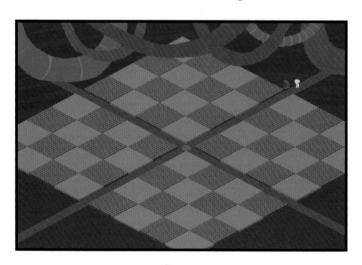

It looks like the kiosk monitors the lab's enormous HUBGRID.

> Jade: Transportalize as far down as you can go.

Oh my god. The hubgrid looks like a chess board. I JUST noticed that!!!

Ha ha, just messin' with you. I made it that way on purpose. Can't believe you actually fell for that.

This is as far down as you can go.

The GRAND FOYER is still a few floors down, but the TRANSPORTALIZER on that level is blocked by one of GRANDPA'S impressive BIG GAME TROPHIES, and you just don't think he would cotton to someone moving it.

Speaking of which, here are some of his TROPHIES now. He has a million of these ghastly things. You really dislike them.

> Jade: Proceed.

You hop down a level.

Granddad also likes to accumulate VALIANT KNIGHTS from his travels. These are pretty cool, you guess.

> Jade: Keep going.

Jade's parental unit, as the Pattern Breaking parental unit, has a much larger variety of strange, off-putting interests. Dad has FANCIFUL HARLEQUINS, Mom has EXQUISITE WIZARDS, and Bro has RADICAL PUPPETS. Grandpa has not one, but FOUR such interests of the same descriptive two-word format. They're all just as dumb, though. One reason among several for this variety was to create an element of uncertainty over what kind of item Jade would prototype with. And by uncertainty, I mean misdirection, which is what I always mean by uncertainty.

Oh yeah. How could you forget about his stash of DECREPIT MUMMIES.

God you hate these things.

> Jade: Don't stop.

Notice the colors of the lights in each room. Orange, pink, and cyan, corresponding to Dirk, Roxy, and Jane. The items have a loose correlation with the other three guardians too. Knights in that Dirk is a skilled swordsman. Roxy's land is full of pyramids. Jane was Grandpa's long-estranged blue lady. You see how the gears are always turning. Not only does everything mean something, it turns out everything means EVERYTHING. Now you know.

This is your grandfather's collection of what he refers to as his BEAUTIES. No lovely lady will be fit for his collection unless her portrait has spent at least 20 years bleaching in the front window of a beauty parlor, a sort of establishment he's plundered no less frequently than ancient tombs.

You guess they were sort of like your sisters while growing up, and you were always encouraged to look up to them. They are all awfully pretty ladies you suppose, but it was always hard to get as excited about them as grandpa.

"Jade, study hard and keep your rifle at the ready. When adventure summons, I know you will rise to the task and take your rightful place among the DAUGHTERS OF ECLECTICA."

That old coot sure is a bag of wind!

> Jade: Complete your descent.

The beauties were the oddest of the four oddball interests, to say the least. I'm just going to observe this struck me as a novel and hilarious fetish. Also, I defy you to enter a beauty parlor or hair salon or such without seeing one or more posters hanging up that have been bleached due to years of exposure to the sun. Something about the chemistry of CMYK inks I guess makes the yellow and magenta inks degrade in sunlight faster than blue ink. Or maybe technology has advanced and this doesn't happen anymore? Maybe I'm just as much of a dinosaur as Grandpa.

You reach the ground level. This is the stupid thing blocking the transportalizer. It is unspeakably hideous.

Down the southeast hall is the GRAND FOYER. You'll have to cross through it to leave the house.

Looks like someone's pestering you.

Even though you thought you logged off... ?

> Jade: Answer.

Referring to this creature as "unspeakably hideous" is probably the funniest joke in the book so far. From now on, I'm going to tell you which jokes are funny. Is that understood? Okay, great.

carcinoGeneticist [CG] began trolling gardenGnostic [GG] at 13:04

CG: HI AGAIN, IDIOT.
GG: oh nooooooo
CG: SO I GUESS TODAY IS FINALLY THE DAY YOU FUCK EVERYTHING UP.
GG: >:O
CG: IS THERE NOTHING I CAN DO TO CHANGE YOUR MIND?
GG: you can leave me alone!!!!!
GG: how can you even be talking to me after i blocked you....
GG: AND after i logged out????
CG: YOU DON'T GET THAT I AM BETTER AND SMARTER THAN YOU IN EVERY WAY, FOREVER.
CG: YOU DON'T GET THAT BECAUSE YOU ARE INCREDIBLY STUPID.
GG: i get that youre a jerk and you should shut up!
GG: goodbye you jerk!!!!!!!!!

gardenGnostic [GG] blocked carcinoGeneticist [CG] at 13:06

> Rose: Look at that kiosk.

Here's Karkat. He's an asshole. He will be this obnoxious loudmouth popping into the story to shout some nonsense every now and then for the next several hundred pages, until we finally learn his name (which is Karkat) in Act 5. But then later you will grow to love him, as he exhibits qualities which are somehow more human than most other characters, which is ironic, because he is not a human. Oh, I should have mentioned: in addition to telling you which jokes are funny, I'm also going to tell you which characters are good. I am a really helpful author.

```
SN_HUBGRID 44.519872,-74.820017

0000   0144   0288   0432       2496   2640   2784   2928
0143   0287   0431   0575       2639   2783   2927   3071

0576   0720   0864   1008       3072   3216   3360   3504
0719   0863   1007   1151       3215   3359   3503   3647

1152   1296   1440   1584       3648   3792   3936   4080
1295   1439   1583   1727       3791   3935   4079   4223

1728   1872   2016   2160       4224   4368   4512   4656
1871   2015   2159   2303       4367   4511   4655   4799

5200   5344   5488   5632       7696   7840   7984   8128
5343   5487   5631   5775       7839   7983   8127   8271

5776   5920   6064   6208       8272   8416   8560   8704
5919   6063   6207   6351       8415   8559   8703   8847

6352   6496   6640   6784       8848   8992   9136   9280
6495   6639   6783   6927       8991   9135   9279   9423

6928   7072   7216   7360       9424   9568   9712   9856
7071   7215   7359   7503       9567   9711   9855   9999

> unlock SN_LAB0413
>|
```

Looks like a mapping of each hub's index.

It appears one of the hubs was recently unlocked.

> Rose: Go to the center and do a goofy dance.

At the center, you find a little stage that looks perfect for supporting a spectacularly silly dance. Or it would if standing on it didn't make you a little nervous, and also if that didn't sound like a retarded idea given the circumstances.

It looks sort of like the various contraptions you've been deploying in John's house. You wonder what it does?

> Rose: Attempt to plug laptop into nearby hub.

All of those blocks in the 8x8 grids are numbered correctly, which as I recall was a fairly painstaking process. There are exactly 10,000 tiny squares there (each representing a green power cube), but each block is 12x12, and the vertical/horizontal paths of four squares wide are subtracted from the 10,000 total, so the numbers weren't very even. Oh, also take note of the GPS coordinates, which point to a real place in upstate New YoAUGH WHY IS EVERYTHING SO NUMERICALLY METICULOUS, OH MY GOD, ROSE PLEASE JUST DO SOMETHING FUNNY AND DISTRACT ME FROM THIS PEDANTIC NIGHTMARE I HAVE CREATED.

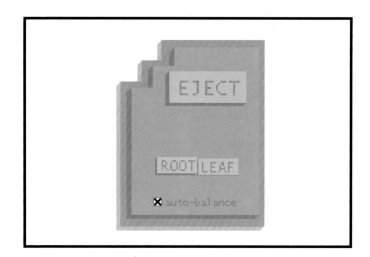

Great, you just vaporized your dead cat.
Oh well. Ashes to ashes you guess.

There's got to be a better way to
deal with this lousy tree.

> Rose: Examine fetch modus.

Looks like you can choose between
picking leaves, or awkwardly uprooting
the whole tree, as you've been doing.

You select LEAF. You also turn off
AUTO-BALANCE, since its consequences
can be a little mystifying sometimes.

Look, Rose is cooperating by doing some funny stuff. Thank you for saving me from my meltdown, Rose. Random musing: if I were to go about editing this story, how critical do you think it would be to leave in the part about auto-balancing the tree modus? I don't know, it might be too important. Better keep it. In fact, it might be prudent to insert another five or six pages pseudocoding the auto-balancing algorithm, just so we really know what we're dealing with here.

You gather up all your items again in an order that places your LAPTOP in a conveniently accessible leaf. You're not sure why you didn't do this a lot sooner.

Kind of a funny looking tree now, but your concern for structural elegance is at an all time low.

> Rose: Find the unlocked hub.

As long as you're going to plug in your computer, you might as well find that hub.

Here it is. HUB SN_LAB0413. It is unlocked, and thus removable from the grid.

You suspect this was the same beacon transmitting the unsecured signal you were using earlier.

You pick the LAPTOP leaf from the tree.

The carapacians who ran this facility when it was in the Veil had a real problem with people sneaking into the place and stealing the hubs, so they made this whole system where the hubs were all locked to the floor and could only be unlocked by the kiosk. That way, if you wanted to steal some hubs, you had to get in line behind everyone waiting to use the kiosk, unlock your hubs, and steal them one at a time in an orderly manner.

You plug your LAPTOP into the HUB, then captchalogue the HUB and then the LAPTOP.

There must be a better place around here to set up your computer.
This huge grid of electronics is sort of uninviting. You look around.

Hey, what's that?

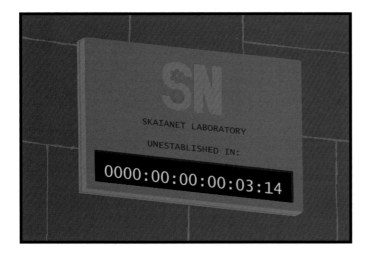

It's another one of these ominous countdowns. You didn't notice it when you first entered the lab about a minute ago. It looks like this one may have been ticking for years.

Whatever it's ticking down to, there isn't much time. You can only hope that when you turn on your computer again, there will be a connection invitation from one Mr. Strider.

> Again in the future...

"UNESTABLISHED IN" is a common type of phrase you see in cultures whose mythology and traditions revolve around the apocalypse. They are much more fixated on endings than beginnings. Their fairytales never start with "Once upon a time..." They usually start with something like "Once, long before everyone died..."

73

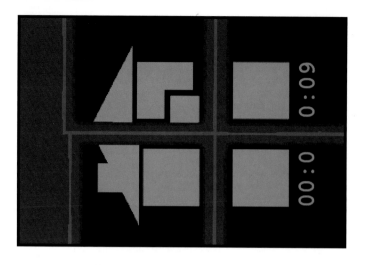

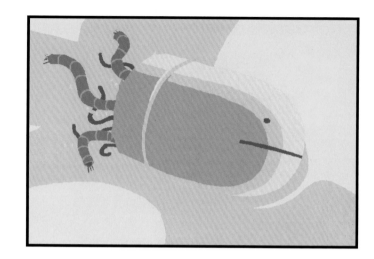

Another timer winds down, sideways.

When PM's impressive TALLNESS ATTRIBUTE is still a heap of mailboxes short of getting the job done, then you know the situation is seriously fucked.

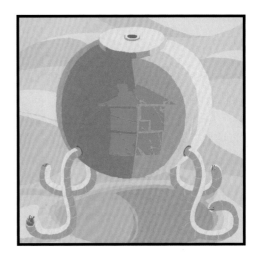

>[S] Dave: Abscond.

The PM x Sentry Worm Best Friendship Forever got off to kind of a rocky start when she decapitated him. But it's cool, there are three more, so she gets a do-over.

In Round 2 of Dave's strife, he tries to escape from the relentless puppet pummeling, but Bro slashes the ABSCOND command, just like he sliced all the other battle commands in Round 1. The message is clear: Dave can't escape until he has been dealt the requisite daily helping of domestic abuse—wait, I mean ninja training. What did I say there? Nothing. It was nothing. *Homestuck* is a lighthearted and funny cartoon dealing in highly abstract and stylized household situations, and nothing about it shall evoke the gritty realities experienced every day by real-life victims of abuse. Now let's watch this thirty-something-year-old man pound the daylights out of his adopted thirteen-year-old brother and biological son.

Dave is like. You see this. This foam puppet I guess I decapitated earlier when I flipped out in the kitchen. See it. Yeah. This could be you. Just watch your step Bro.

Professional tip: use the blur filter to make it look like someone is going fast. Am I the first person to ever think of that neat trick? The answer is, almost certainly.

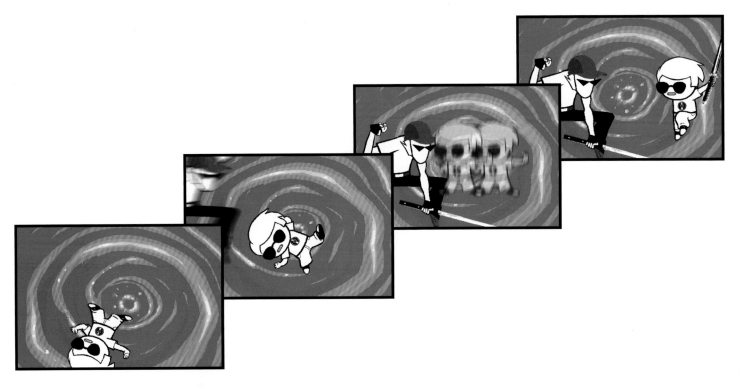

Bro is really just pissed at Dave for ripping up the weird *Muppet Babies* comic that was taped to the door.

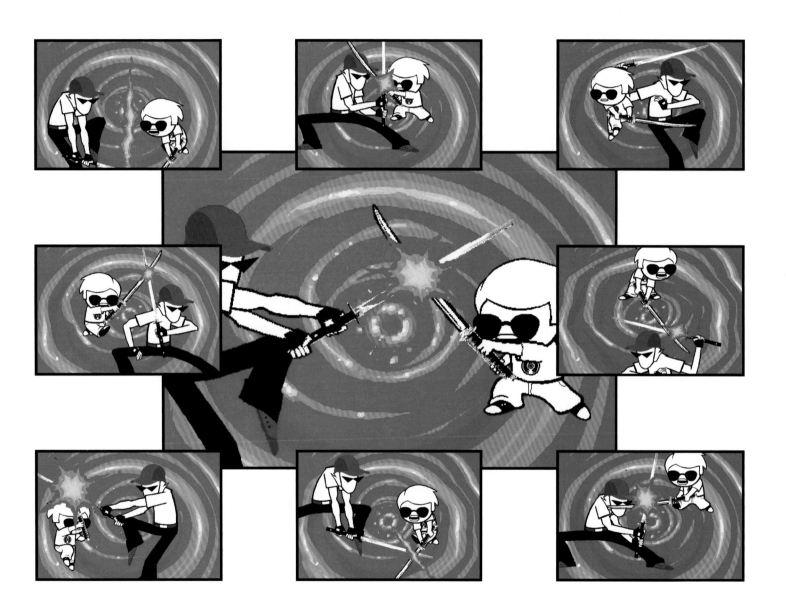

If a dude is in a sword fight, he cannot be authoritatively identified as an ice-cold motherfucker unless he blocks the other guy's sword without even looking.

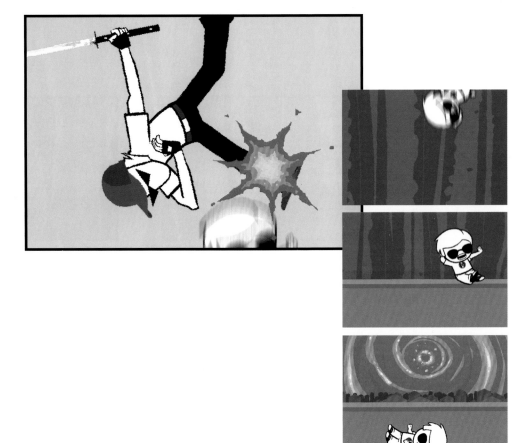

It is also an unwritten rule that in nonlethal sword fights, while all the coolest moves are done through swordplay, any attack that makes any actual bodily contact must be done through punching and kicking. That's because in reality, if a sword slices you, you pretty much just die. And when someone dies, that's when the coolness ends. Although I guess theoretically one of the swordsmen could still sort of leap and cavort around the dead body, flipping out awesomely with his sword and such. That would be one way to prolong an awesome sword fight.

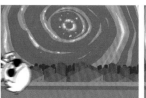
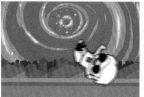

Dave was doing all right there for a while, but here's where it all starts to unravel. Don't worry, the training is for your own good, Dave. It comes in handy later when you...uh...I guess when you swindle some idiot crocodiles out of trillions of dollars in the stock market?

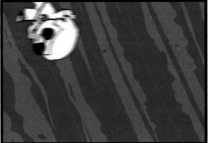

Let's face facts. This training was pretty much useless.

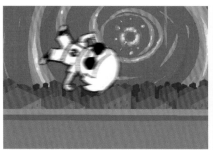
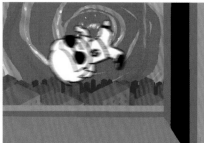

Bro is just standing there with Cal, who's primed for the knockout blow with his tiny hightop sneaker. Insult, meet injury. Again, hang in there, Dave. You will get your revenge later in the story, by grieving over your older brother's slain, bloody corpse.

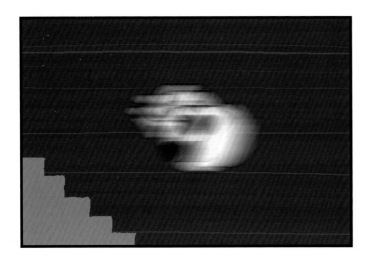

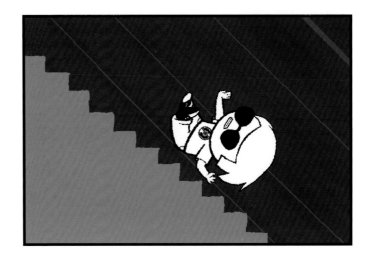

> IT KEEPS HAPPENING

There are many, many references to *Sweet Bro and Hella Jeff* throughout *Homestuck*, both visual and textual. Each one serves a very important purpose. That purpose is usually to remind you that *Sweet Bro and Hella Jeff* exists. Especially if you don't like it.

What does?

You don't have time to humor every random thought that pops into your head. The clock is ticking.

> Rose: Look around for anything else of importance.

This looks like something of importance.

It appears to be Skaianet's primary SESSION TERMINAL, monitoring a great number of SBURB SESSIONS in the northeastern United States and parts of Canada. Upon further investigation you draw some logical conclusions.

It looks like each SESSION consists of an IP address and a physical location. The colored dots on the map appear to be METEOR IMPACT SITES. It seems each session corresponds with a meteor, but not all meteors have sessions.

The color of the dot appears to indicate the status of the meteor's descent. The red dots indicate meteors that have already landed. Yellow dots are imminent collisions. Green will impact later, and blue will take the longest to touch down.

There is a lot of trivia to talk about here. But most of the trivia is already covered by the narration. That's the great thing about *Homestuck*. Whenever something weird or confusing is going on in a panel, a lot of times it's just straight-up fucking EXPLAINED underneath, using a whole bunch of words. That's the key to good storytelling. Just explain everything. No, stop laughing at me. Shut up. But for real, here's some trivia. In the lower panel, on one of the right-hand screens, see that small diagram of an eight-planet session? That's probably the most obscure and long-term bit of foreshadowing in the entire story.

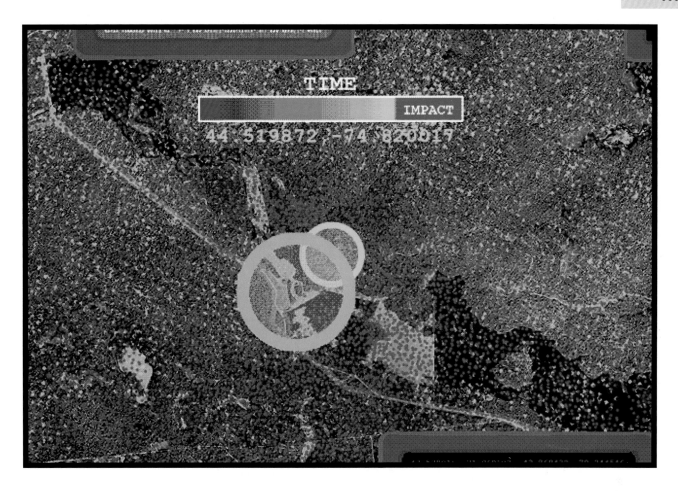

You use the panel to center on your present location and zoom in. Surrounding the lab are of course the hundreds of smaller meteors that have been raining down steadily throughout the evening. Most of these meteor(ite)s have either landed already, or will shortly.

Centered over the lab is a significantly larger imminent collision. You can't say precisely how imminent, but you could certainly take an educated stab at it.

Just southwest of the lab, centered suspiciously near the location of your house, is an even larger looming collision. Though this one appears slightly less imminent.

The terminal looks like it can monitor any meteor or session around the world. Search filters can be applied as well, restricting results based on size, time of impact, location, and so on.

I wonder if one of those little meteors landed squarely on the Burger King about a half hour north of Rose's house, which Rose and Dave talk about like 3,000 pages later. For some reason this strikes me as a sad thought.

You zoom way out and narrow the search based on size. The two at the top of the list appear to be the biggest by far. You examine only their coordinates.

The second biggest is centered over a U.S. city. The biggest by a landslide is, luckily for the Earth you suppose, way out in the middle of the Pacific ocean.

> Rose: Turn on your laptop and check on John.

You plug the laptop into the hub again and turn it on. It is now powered and connected to the wireless signal the hub is broadcasting.

Your Sburb session reconnects.

No sign of John here. You wonder why the house is shaking.

Last time you saw him he was on one of the roof platforms. You will have to navigate via the Sburb interface to find him.

>[S] Rose: Ascend.

OBVIOUS TRIVIA ZONE! The green circle hovers over Dave's city, which appears to be somewhere in Texas. Does Dave being a Texan make him a better or funnier character? I'll leave that conclusion to you. The huge blue circle signifying the Extinction Level Event impact is targeting Jade's island. But don't worry. With Earth's First Guardian protecting the planet, what could go wrong?

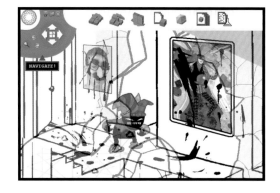
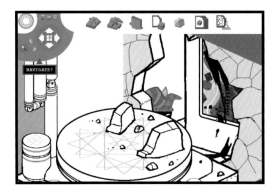

The reader has to use the *Sburb* interface to navigate through the house to find John. Which really just serves as an intro to the second round of RUMBLE ON DA ROOF! Starting John, Nanna, some ogres, and now Rose at the *Sburb* helm.

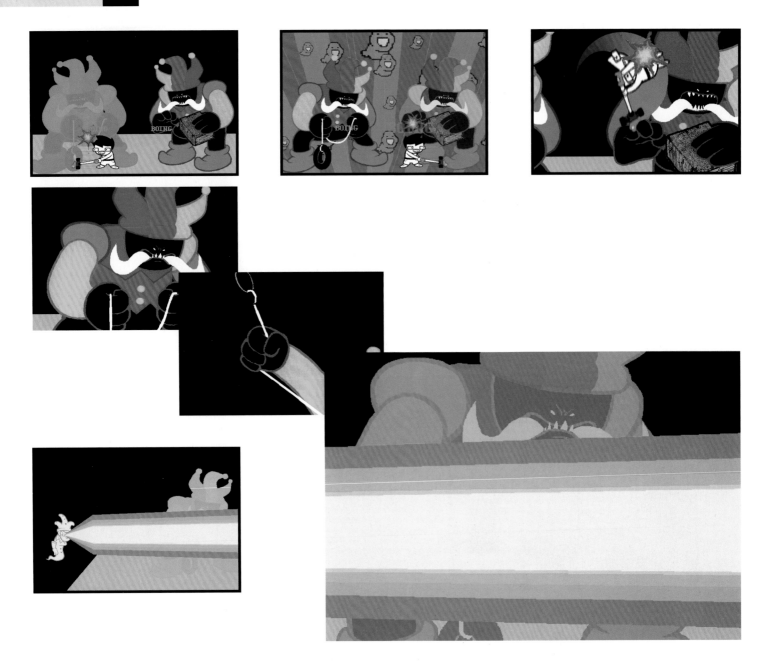

With a little help, John does better this time. That's because the most important themes of *Homestuck* are teamwork and friendship. In fact, the most important themes of every work of fiction are teamwork and friendship. Don't ever be fooled into thinking otherwise.

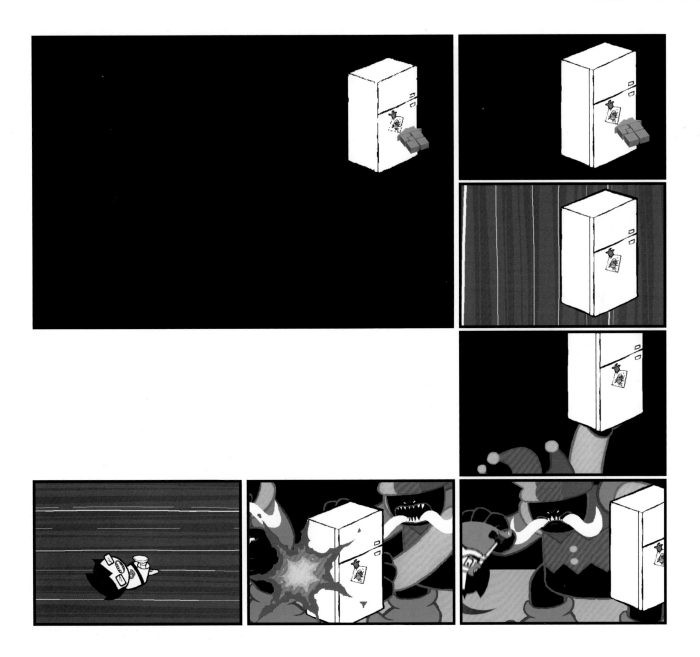

John takes a hunger trunk to the kisser. This is what John's dad would regard as a quality character-building experience. If he were watching, he would be stroking his chin in fatherly approval.

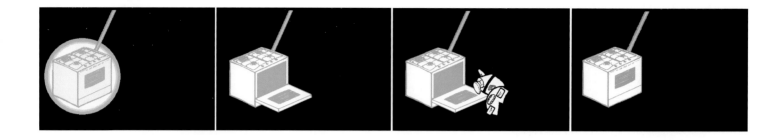

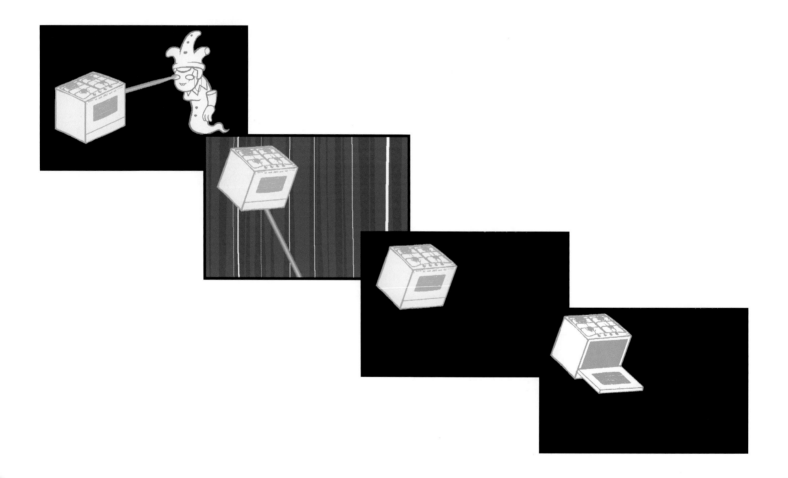

Nanna's phantom oven doubles as a GRANDSON LAUNCHER. Actually, there are more ovens that physically contain characters in the story than there are ovens that don't.

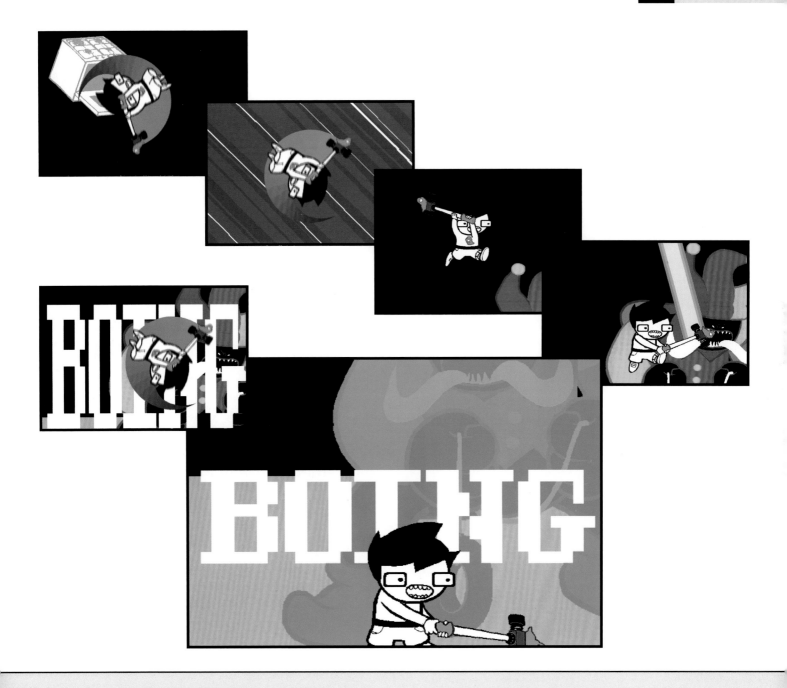

This attack is so KINETIC in the animation. Specifically, that BOING is just so BOINGY. Seeing it here like this, it's so static and lifeless, it's like watching a caged bird yearning to spread its wings and wow I am being melodramatic.

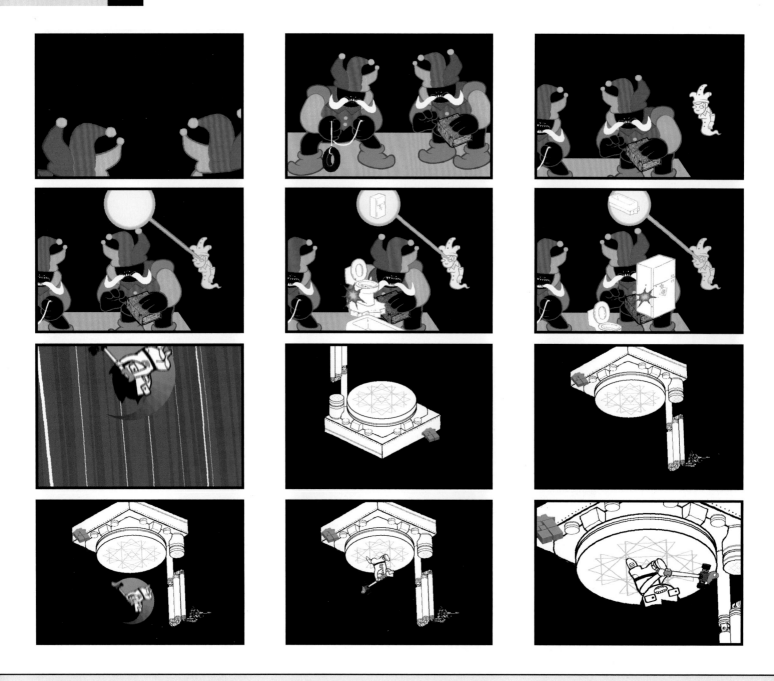

Sometimes these animations were so fast-paced, they could be a little hard to follow. It's a relief to see that when slowed down and printed frame by frame in a book, they're barely any easier to follow at all.

Cue the shot of John connecting with a Pogo Hammer blow while a random bathtub is in frame behind him.

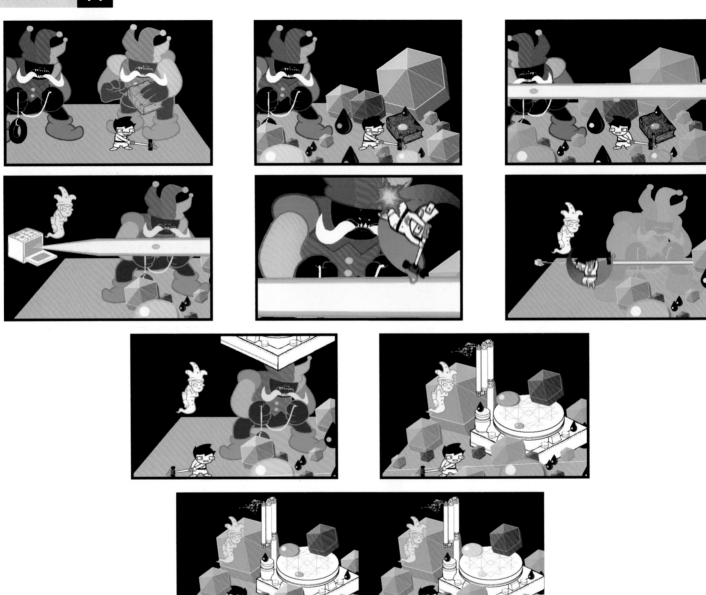

> John: High-five Nannaquin.

LOOK AT ALL THAT GODDAMN GRIST. One of the keys to showing advancement through a long mock-game in the form of an illustrated story is to not show every grueling milestone of achievement, every level gained or every treasure collected, but to at least show major incremental advancements are POSSIBLE. Like so. And then the imagination can fill in the blanks with many more of the types of windfalls we just saw. So later, when we see John sitting on a huge pile of grist, we can just say, oh yeah, looks like John killed about a thousand ogres for all that loot.

LEFT HANGING
LONG ENOUGH

TT: Good work, John!
EB: oh, hey!
EB: you're back.
TT: For now. I'll have to leave again shortly.
TT: It looks like there's another large meteor headed for...
TT: My present location.
EB: oh, so you mean dave connected with you?
TT: Not yet.
TT: I'll explain later.
TT: But I think I've determined that activating the timer in the game is not directly responsible for summoning a meteor to your location.
TT: The countdown seems merely to exist as a kind of warning to the player.
TT: As well as a strange coincidence.
EB: um, ok.
EB: i don't really think i get it.
EB: is this relevant?
TT: Probably not at the moment. And certainly not to you.
TT: I have to go.
EB: ok, later!
TT: P.S. Try not to waste too much of that grist while I'm gone.

> John: Climb that echeladder.

John: Immediately waste all that grist on a shiny new fleet of pogo rides and ten tons of Gushers.

You rocket up the ECHELADDER to the dizzying heights of the vaunted BOY-SKYLARK rung!!! Your new feather is hard earned and well deserved. And alarmingly fashionable.

> John: Collect phat lewtz.

You and your CERAMIC PORKHOLLOW rejoice in the mound of wealth yielded from your meteoric ascent up the ladder.

You are still not sure what all these BOONDOLLARS can actually get you. But when pulling in such insane loot hand over fist like this, who cares?

Not you.

> John: Pick up as much grist as you can hold.

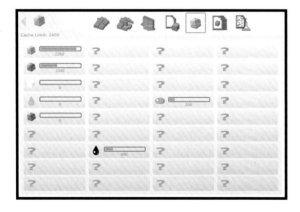

Your expanded CACHE LIMIT is more than enough to accommodate the grist windfall.

You gather up 2260 pieces of BUILD GRIST, 1040 pieces of SHALE, 490 drops of TAR, and 350 drops of MERCURY.

You can't wait to find out what amazing items this new supply of grist will be just barely insufficient to produce.

It's too bad John skipped over the GADABOUT PIPSQUEAK rung entirely. That was the level that contained puberty.

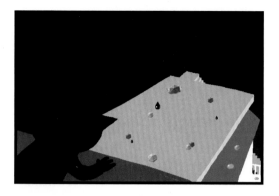

Oh god, there's grist littered down there too. Those stupid ogres were like huge grist pinatas.

One of those big SOUR GRAPE ELECTRIC HOLOCAUST FRUIT GUSHERS is jammed in the hole in the platform. You guess there's only one way to get it.

NANNASPRITE: John, don't forget your book!
NANNASPRITE: It is your birthright! You ought to give it a read when you have a moment. Particularly the first several pages!
JOHN: ok nanna, i will.
JOHN: hey, nanna?
NANNASPRITE: Yes, dear?
JOHN: since i am trying to get up to that gate, and since you can sort of conjure floating beds and throw me around and all...
JOHN: couldn't you just throw me up to the gate?
NANNASPRITE: Yes, of course, John!
NANNASPRITE: But that would not serve your purpose well!
NANNASPRITE: There is a very good reason why you should build up to it. And then keep building!
JOHN: oh, ok, i guess that's what i figured.
JOHN: so just one more thing...
JOHN: do you think that instead of telling me exactly why that is with a clear explanation, you can give me a series of really coy riddles about it and then sort of giggle?
NANNASPRITE: John, you are a very fresh young man!
NANNASPRITE: Your father has done such a wonderful job raising you. I am so proud of you both.
JOHN: ha ha, i guess.
NANNASPRITE: When you pass through the first gate, everything will change. You will find the place where the constellations dance beneath the clouds. And then your true work may begin.
NANNASPRITE: Hoo hoo hoo!
JOHN: i suddenly understand everything!

> Elsewhere, we find a place...

Little Known Fact, soon to be a Widely Known Fact: any time I spell a foreign word that has a special character in it, like piñata, I never bother with the 'ñ.' I always just go with the standard 'n.' The way I see it is this. Who cares? Here's an example to help you understand why. Let's say in English, any time you wrote "cool" you had to put a smile under the 'oo' to make it look like a cool guy with sunglasses. If you were a Mexican who had to spell "cool," wouldn't you just say, wow, fuck this, and just spell it without the smile? You're goddamned right you would.

Where a kingdom lies entrenched beyond
an impenetrable veil of darkness.

The first ever drawings of Derse were admittedly pretty funky. I used my standard collaging methods of heavily desaturating and tinting bits and pieces of cathedral architecture, which usually tends to look all right. But then for some reason in these early drawings I kind of scribbled over it with lighter shades of purple. I'm retroactively grading that decision a MEH+.

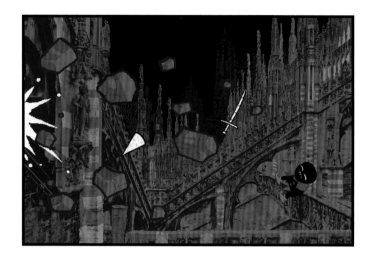

Graveyard stuffers.

> You are now...

Without going into much detail, we MAY be catching a glimpse of the sort of behavior that got Dad banned from the Cirque du Soleil. (He possibly saw a man he deemed too hairy and couldn't control the trigger finger on his lather blaster... I'VE SAID TOO MUCH ALREADY.)

The Peregrine Mendicant.

You are flying westward in your peculiar mobile station. You have no sense of your bearings presently. The door is blocked by a metal column which extended through the entry shaft before liftoff.

What will you do?

> PM: Check mail.

This message to Dr. Brinner looks pretty serious.

> PM: Open envelope.

NEVER.

The mail is sacred, and sacred is the trust between the Post Man and the recipients of his precious parcels. You have made a solemn pledge to deliver this letter to the doctor, just as soon as you determine where this address is, or find any sort of discernible mailing address in this wasteland, for that matter. The mail is freedom. The mail is life. The mail is the very fabric of civiliz...

Wait.

Hold that thought for one moment...

Some readers used to pretend I did another story starring a guy named Dr. David Brinner, and they made up a bunch of bullshit about the story and made a TV Tropes page for it and everything. So I decided to address this envelope to him. This gesture seems a little silly to me in retrospect, because by now there is so much bogus fanon lore about my creations and the things I've done, it's barely worth keeping track of, let alone acknowledging in the story. Also, pay attention to that postage stamp. It'll show up again later. Oh who am I kidding, you're going to forget I ever mentioned it.

The mail is the one final hope for resurrecting a dead planet from its ashes, and the letter carriers are the brave soldiers of God in this righteous crusade. They are the defenders of the light of knowledge, free communication, and the exchange of ideas. They are the bold toters of all those little papery conduits of freedom, the white postmarked angels that whisper a message on their deliverance, a promise to the yearning: "There is hope yet."

Liberty. Reason. Justice. Civility. Edification. Perfection.

MAIL.

> PM: Examine keyboard and screen.

Gosh, the Perigrine Mendicant sure does love her some mail. Alternatively, this entire page can be read as me ripping on Costner's film *The Postman*, whose nearly fetishistic portrayal of mail delivery as the backbone of civilization was, to be honest, just a bit silly. *The Postman* was based on a novel of the same title that was written, fascinatingly, by a man named David Brin. He has a Ph.D. Yes, that is Dr. David Brin. I guarantee that you are floored by this utterly magical coincidence.

It's the terminal you used to activate the station's homing mechanism. It looks like it has now returned control to you.

The default viewport displays commands previously entered, including your last and only command "=> HOME".

> PM: Type => VIEW

You type another one of the previously entered commands. It switches to the view of a young girl standing alone somewhere. There is a heavy amount of video interference of some sort.

The girl seems familiar to you.

> Greetings.

> Don't I know you?

Another maddening glimpse of the future. When the station terminals are first used, they're cued up to the moments shortly after the kid onscreen has entered the Medium. PM is Jade's exile. Though sadly, she doesn't get to play that role for very long.

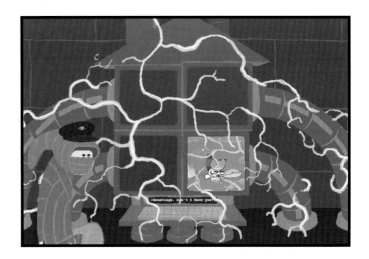

We are invited to wonder many things. What's that on the ground? Is it ash from an erupting volcano? Is it snow? Why is Jade shaking her head at the camera? Does she know PM is there? Are her "psychic abilities" in play? Is that also why the thing blew up?? Like I said. Maddening. Stay tuned to find out what really happened in 2,000 pages.

> Rose: Refuse to acknowledge the absurd tea set.

You successfully disregard the TEA SET because it's stupid and shouldn't be in a place like this. You probe further into the lab.

Looks like a little girl's room.
This all strikes you as a bit odd.

No time for messing around in here though.

> Rose: Wear the scarf. Be the Rider.

It never even comes close to being explicated in the story, but it is strongly implied that this is where Rose's mom grew up. Though after the introduction of Roxy, and another reread, this probably becomes more obvious. Who raised her? Was it the owner of Skaianet, a younger Grandpa Harley? Did he outsource parenting duties to someone else in the lab? Maybe some exiles? If so, she had an upbringing fairly similar to that of Roxy in the future. These mysteries have LEGS.

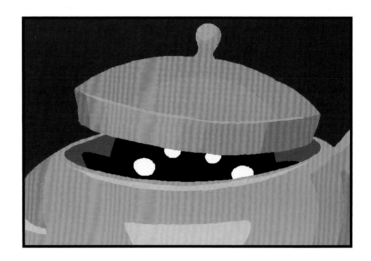

Ok, maybe you'll do a LITTLE messing around. You are only human after aAUGH WHAT'S THAT

You are accosted by a friendly MUTANT KITTEN.

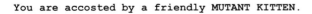

> John: Resist great urge to take the wedged shale.

You know you should grab this thing, but...

John: Never mind that big purple Gusher. Look up and say hi to Vodka Mutini.

You are suddenly feeling apprehensive about entering your father's room. With all the scamperin' around it almost slipped your mind how much you hate his hideous clowns.

No use putting it off any longer. There is only one thing left to do.

Give me a 'D'.

Give me an 'E'.

Give me an 'S'.

Give me a 'C'...

> John: Jump down.

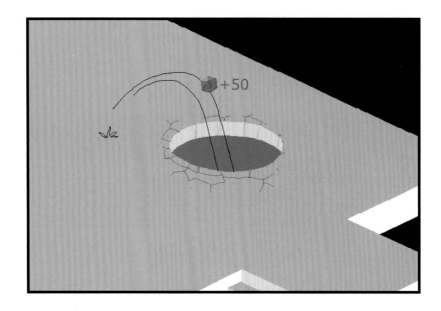

The series of letters up there was going to spell out "Descartes' *Meditationes de prima philosophia, in qua Dei existentia et animæ immortalitas demonstratur*" and was to preface a lengthy treatise on the meditations of the renowned French philosopher. But I decided to cut it short because ultimately it didn't have much to do with John's trepidation about entering his father's room, or his fear of clowns.

> Jade: Scamper into grand foyer with wild abandon.

LASS SCAMPER!

You scamper your heart out and bump into something. You don't know why he always insists on keeping it so dark in here.

Oh look, it was one of his dumb GLOBES. These things make it awfully difficult to navigate the foyer. We get it, granddad. You like to travel around the world going on adventures and stuff!

Lousy goddamn stupid globes.

> Jade: Arm yourself.

GRANDPA will surely have stern words for you if he catches you without your trusty RIFLE at the ready. That's just what you need, another one of his blustering mustachioed diatribes. You are rolling your eyes in advance, getting them warmed up.

But ideally you can evade him altogether. All you have to do is get past the FIREPLACE and out the front door, and you will be scot-free.

> Jade: Examine those chaps on the sofa.

This transition was confusing to some people. At first they thought John had jumped down into this weird room containing a mysterious altar to Jade. But no, this is a scene switch, and that is the foyer of Jade's <SPOILER!> dead </SPOILER!> grandpa. In hindsight, this altar is actually a very poignant memorial to Jade's dream self, who we later discover <SPOILER!> died saving John </SPOILER!> and was <SPOILER!> stuffed by Grandpa /<SPOILER!> and then <SPOILER!> stored in the lab at the top of Jade's house for practically her entire life </SPOILER!>.

These are the manor's four DISTINGUISHED HOUSEGUESTS. They like to gather here by the FIREPLACE for TEA TIME. As well as pretty much all other times. It's all very mannerly and civilized.

You know exactly what's going to happen when you try to sneak by. The FIREPLACE is going to light up and your GRANDPA'S silhouette is going to appear in front of the fire to give you a good spook. He is so predictable.

and there he goes

the old man....
HASS the flame

Consider that these four dolls were basically Old Man Jake's idea of good company to have around the house. The thing you have to understand about Jake is that he's kind of a loner. And also kind of an idiot. Oh well, at least Mr. Moose there looks pretty friendly. Maybe Jake isn't as dumb as he seems. All this probably makes good sense to him. He just has a special kind of brain.

You suppose you could still manage to
sneak by the crafty old man if you are
fast enough. Avoiding an encounter would
be ideal.

Encounters with him are usually........

Intense.

> Jade: Leap dramatically across
the divide.

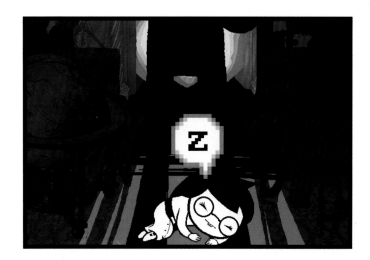

WHOOPS.
You guess an encounter with him is almost certain now.
But most likely not for a while. Time to see what someone else is up to.
Oh, let's say... Dave.

>[S] Strife!!!

VRIIIIIIISKAAAAAAAA!!!!!!!!

</spoiler>

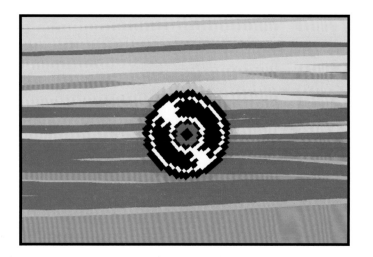

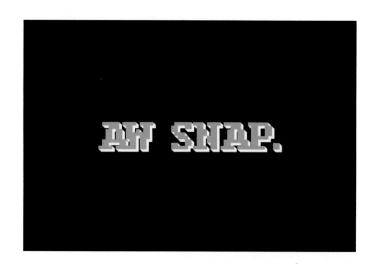

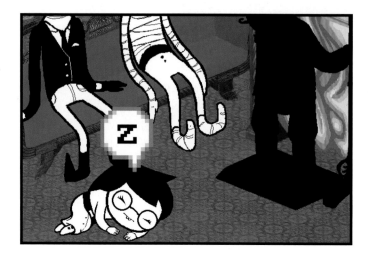

These psycheouts have EVERY OUNCE of punch on paper as they did online, and I won't entertain a single objection to this PERFECT FACT. You thought we were going to watch Dave get puppet whipped some more, but no. It's time to make Jade frolic around the stuffed corpse of her adoptive grandfather and biological father. (Who frankly should just be called her "father" because come on, old dudes are perfectly capable of siring children. This guy is really just "Jade's Dad," end of story.)

Here, just as on the flute page, you can press keyboard keys and make Jade do some totally silly stuff. She likes to pretend to get into strifes with her dead grandpa, which is kinda sad. Also, this is the first page that makes it clear her grandpa was dead all along, thus completing a HUGE TWIST, which is to say, an absolutely miniscule twist in the greater scheme of *Homestuck*. And by "makes it clear he was dead all along," I mean "some people still didn't actually understand he was supposed to be dead here." In fact, I had to go back and draw stitches on his head to make it EXTRA CLEAR, 'cause you know, living people are almost always mounted to plaques bearing their name like a trophy.

YES i am going out with this gun!!! no i will not go get a bigger one!!! no i will not take yours! I can't even lift it!!!!!! oh that is so preposterous. do you even hear what youre saying? i will be fine! this is a perfectly deadly gun and it shoots lots of incredibly deadly bullets! oh will you just stop it. i am going now. Goodbye!!!!!!!!!!!!

<3!!!!!!!!!!!!!!!!!!!!!!!!!!!!!!!

> Jade: Abscond!

He was so much easier to deal
with when he was alive.

> PM: Miraculously survive.

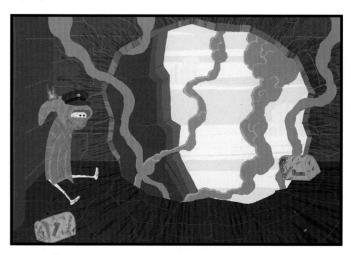

> PM: Peer out explosion hole.

And then to make it EXTRA EXTRA EXTRA EXTRA EXTRA EXTRA EXTRA CLEAR she was just frolicking with a dead man: "He was so much easier to deal with when he was alive." (4,000 pages later I overhear you say, "You know...I'm starting to think Grandpa Harley might have been dead all along!")

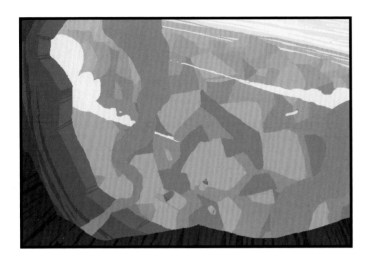

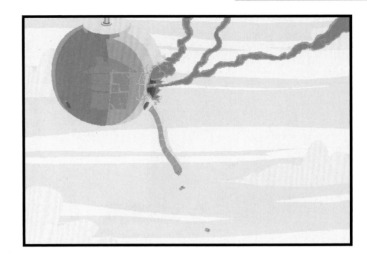

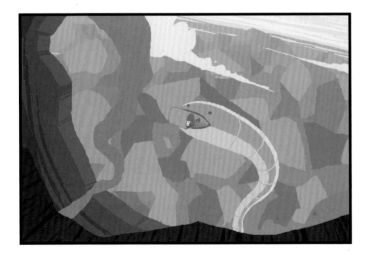

> Rose: Refuse to acknowledge the absurd kitten.

PM x Sentry Worm Best Friendship = BACK ON TRACK!!! But just imagine if PM had decided to use this flying pod to air-drop mail around the wasteland. That overzealous worm would make dropping deliveries SO FRUSTRATING.

You fail miserably.

Oh look, there's some more mad science crap over here.

> Rose: Insert coin.

This weird arcade gizmo adapted to this setup obviously doesn't take coins anymore, assuming it ever did.

Besides, you left all your coins on the fridge, remember?

> Rose: Let's play a game.

This doesn't appear to be a game.

It appears to be an APPEARIFIER.

> Rose: Screw around with the appearifier.

To be fair, if the arcade machine did still take coins, it would probably need more than twelve cents to operate.

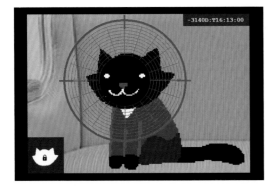

You mess with the controls...

Hey, Jaspers is alive!!!

Or, at least he was in the past. According to the time-stamp this was almost nine years ago.

You try to move the crosshairs with the joystick, but it seems to be permanently locked on a specific target. You might be able to unlock it, but you clearly don't have much time to horse around with this thing.

You zoom out.

It looks like you and Jaspers were having one of your sessions. You weren't making a lot of progress though, because Jaspers was no doubt being characteristically recalcitrant. You possibly jotted this phrase down in your pad. It's hard to remember though.

Wait...

Could this be THAT day??

> Rose: Cause time paradox.

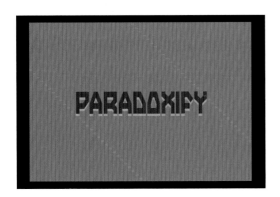

You attempt to appearify Jaspers. This would surely cause a time paradox, because you can plainly see that he has not told you his SECRET yet.

But it seems the machine has a safety mechanism to prevent such irresponsible appearification practices.

Ha ha, Jaspers was being characteristically recalcitrant. That was SO Jaspers.

The PARADOX GHOST IMPRINT of Jaspers appearifies instead, and quickly settles into a mound of sludge.

The machine beside it sucks up the paradox sludge and begins some kind of automated procedure.

It seems whatever sort of primordial biochemical properties the sludge possesses
is being evaluated by the device.

Don't look now, but you are being given a short tutorial in ECTOBIOLOGY. This is important. This is why our heroes exist. Because of slime, temporal mechanics, and fucking around.

The device generates a fetal PARADOX CLONE of Jaspers.

The wretched creature exhibits a number of unfortunate mutations though. The good news is that it will be mercifully UNESTABLISHED along with this facility shortly. This is also the bad news.

Whoever was operating this machine in the past may have been making unsuccessful attempts to perfect the science of ECTOBIOLOGY.

> Rose: Have a flashback.

There is no need for a flashback. Conveniently, you can watch what happened right here on the monitor.

You roll the clock forward a few seconds. Jaspers reveals his stunning SECRET to you in strict confidence.

"Whoever was operating this machine in the past" COUGH MOM. I wonder if in her childhood she made as many cats as she does in the alt-future? Jaspers was surely a result of this process, likely making him a true paradox clone. Bonus facts: Jaspers's secret is, "Yo I'm about to disappear and spend the rest of my life with your mom as a little girl in a water world AU four centuries in the future, then later I'll jet back here as a corpse, and you can attend my funeral which you think your mom is hosting ironically but really isn't."

Before you could ask him to clarify, he vanished into thin air. You now believe you understand why.

However, you were not the one to appearify him from this moment. Your hand was nowhere near the controls just now.

A couple weeks after he vanished, his body washed up along the riverbank. His suit was a mess. Your mother fitted him with a new one just before the absurd funeral service she insisted upon.

> Rose: Trace Jaspers' whereabouts on the machine.

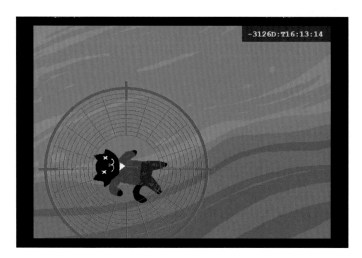

You roll the clock forward to a week after he vanished. It seems there is no accessible feed tracing his whereabouts during that timeframe.

You fast forward another week. There he is, just as you found him.

>[S] Rose: Fast forward to now.

If you ever see time stamps or such in *Homestuck*, just assume I was meticulous about the numbers and try to get on with your life.

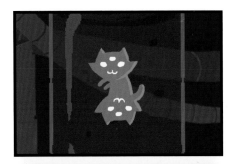

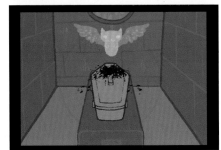

Imagine haunting pipe organ music with an absurd chorus of meows, and you have successfully re-created this animation in your heart. It will live there forever.

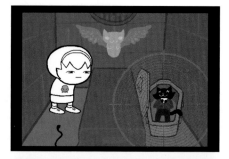

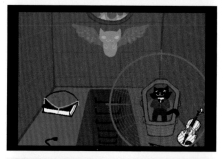

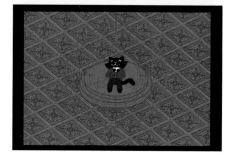

This page has twelve panels. The number of panels featuring new content: two.

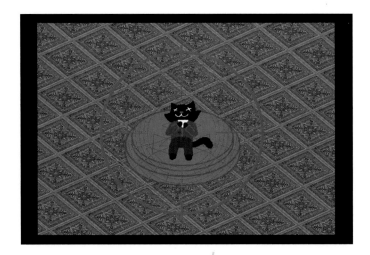

IT'S JASPERS. HE'S ALIVE.

Well ok, he's still dead. But his body is intact. Turns out it wasn't some kind of DISINTEGRATIFICATOR like you thought.

It's more like...

AN ESCAPILIZER.

> Rose: Appearify Jaspers immediately.

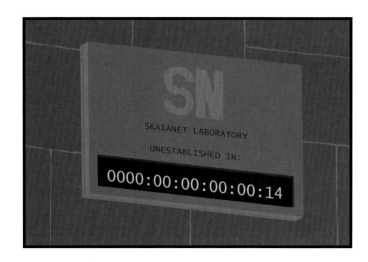

Good thing you finally got all this sorted out. You only have 10 seconds to spare.

Time to stash the dead cat and amscray.

> Rose: Stop fooling around and transportalize out of there!

Rose needs to retrieve Jaspers for important plot reasons. If she hadn't prototyped him later, she would've had no one around to have cute conversations with.

PRETTY DECENT ESCAPALIZATION

> Jade: Locate and feed the devilbeast you call a pet.

Good luck finding him! If he wants to be found, he will find you.

Becquerel has always managed to elude your prognosticative faculties. He is completely invisible to your intuition somehow, a property almost totally unique to him.

It used to freak you out a little, but you have long since grown accustomed to it.

We don't know here yet that Jade's "intuition" is mostly tied to her dreams on Prospit, so when the text here says that Bec is "invisible" to her intuition I guess that's mostly code for "she never dreams about him." This is because, at the risk of becoming excessively technical, First Guardians are really, really mysterious.

HUH???

Oh, it was nothing. Nothing at all.
Moving right along.

> Jade: Retrieve the package you expected
to arrive.

The birthday package you were expecting from John
arrived months late. And yet, right on time.

It landed over there past the crumbling monument,
a satellite to the great MYSTIC RUINS at the
center of the CRATER LAGOON.

> John: Triple somersault into room, etc.
Stick the landing.

Becquerel had to bolt suddenly because someone on the other side of the world just threw a tennis ball.

Ok, you do that. You are now in your DAD'S room.

Hmm... Where are all the clowns?

You spot your DAD'S BRIEFCASE beside you. It probably contains all sorts of clues, or at least various forms and paperwork critical to his trade as a hilarious street performer.

> John: Snoop.

Aw yeah, here come the secrets. Get ready for some MAJOR revela...

Wait a minute. These are just boring business documents and spreadsheets.

What the hell is going on here???

>[S] John: Examine your dad's room.

John's dismay is compounded when he scans the spreadsheets and realizes his dad's boring firm got hammered in the fourth quarter.

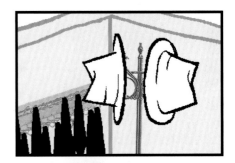

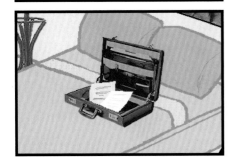

Imagine for a moment that this page WASN'T an animation set to some extremely dramatic over-the-top music for the sake of laughs. Just imagine that instead I deliberately composed this sequence of panels specifically for a book, exactly like this. What a surreal and marvelously peculiar display of sequential art. Actually, thinking about it like this somehow makes the joke funnier.

> John: Calm down, it'll be alright.

I don't know what kind of father doesn't have a series of pipes mounted on his bedroom wall, just above a lone box of cake mix in the corner.

Maybe Hitler's father. I dunno.

So all those years, while you believed he was out busking up the corners with hilarious antics, he was working as an ordinary business man all along. He was just a man trying to make a good honest living for his son. Maybe he was too embarrassed to tell you the truth? Or maybe it was just that you'd never bothered to ask?

You guess you always just assumed...

The human prisoner has broken out of his jail cell yet again. Attempts to block the cell door with heavy objects have proven futile.

Unrevealed fact: when John imagined his dad's life as a street busker, he figured most people who gave him money were paying him to stop.

You're going to need a bigger safe.

Who's this guy?

> Enter name.

Jack. That man is why you are forced to wear that ridiculous outfit. If he hadn't pretended to love clowns to bond with his son, he wouldn't have bought the clown doll, and Rose wouldn't have prototyped it, thus imbuing your queen with clowniness, thus making her insist that everyone in the kingdom wear clownish attire. Jack, are you listening? He stopped listening halfway through that explanation because it was boring.

Spades Slick?

Got a nice ring to it.

But you know your own name. And that damn well ain't your name.

> Take another stab at it.

Ok.

> State name and rank.

The orange fingers are my fingers. Why are they orange? Let's not answer that question. Next question. Why are my fingers typing a guess at Jack's name, and then commanding him to state his name and rank? Jack at this stage is the villain. Villains in *Homestuck* tend to be metavillains. That is, they exist much closer to the surface of the story's metabubble and often interact with the way it's told. For instance, Jack Noir is the original owner of the Fourth Wall. (See next page.) As a universal bureaucratic game construct, he can keep tabs on everything going on in the session, including just outside the story.

You are ARCHAGENT JACK NOIR. You oversee various affairs of a DARK KINGDOM. Presently you are determining how to deal with this prisoner, who has been a thorn in your side since he was apprehended.

You view the affairs of the kingdom through a series of FENESTRATED WALLS. You have three walls, nearly enough to form a CUBICLE OF VIGILANCE, which is a full and proper enclosure for an agent of your stature.

However, much to your utter contempt, your FOURTH WALL was stolen some time ago.

> Jack: Don comical hat.

Though Jack Noir is a metavillain, there are limits to this role, possibly tied to his personality. It could be that the scope of his ambition never includes messing with the story itself. His desire for power lies entirely within fictional parameters. Later, there are much more flagrant metavillains in Doc Scratch and Lord English. They live on the surface of the metabubble and at times badly puncture it. All iterations of Lord English in sum essentially represent the ultimate metavillain. Though it takes a very long time for this to become apparent and for its exact meaning to be revealed.

This frivolous headdress turns your stomach. You'd sooner stick your head in a furnace than coax it into this monstrosity's loathsome colorful maw.

It's bad enough that your EXALTED RULER ordered everyone to drape themselves in these hideous rags the moment the troublesome human with the pipe and his child showed up.

But you draw the line at the hat.

> Jack: Call a minion.

You order one of your burliest agents to the scene. He brings something heavier this time.

Hearts Boxcars, a.k.a. the Hegemonic Brute, despite being the muscle of Jack's crew, is repeatedly proven to be the whipping boy of the agents. He just keeps getting his ass handed to him. And the deeper we get into the story, the shorter-lived his instances are.

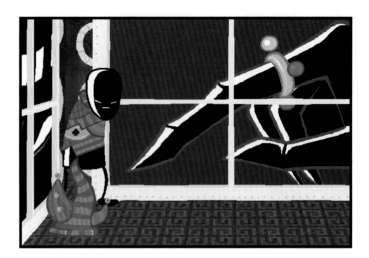

Your transmission is interrupted.

It seems your GLORIOUS MONARCH has concerns over your wardrobe.

FINE.

You begrudgingly don the COMICAL HAT.

Stupid lousy WISE AND JUST LEADER.
What a royal pain in the ass.

> Jack: Throw down hat in disgust.

"Glorious Monarch," huh. Gotta be a dude, right? Nope, that's the queen. Come to think of it, this turns out to be a minor trend. Later there's a character named Snowman, and we're all like, come on now that has GOT to be a dude. But NOPE, it's the Black Queen yet again. PM turning out to be a girl I guess maybe is part of this trend too, but that was literally only a surprise because she had neither boobs nor "girl eyelashes."

WHOMP

You fully intend to once your superior stops
breathing down your neck for a second.

Wait...

What now?

Your blood is boiling so hot you could cook an
egg on your carapace.

Looks like you'll have to go handle this yourself.

> John: Investigate room for anything dad
may have left behind

The ongoing humiliation of HB begins. Also let us note...wait hold on /temporarily unblocks tvtropes.org from browser, goes there/ okay yes, let us note the "Worf Effect"
taking place here. Earlier, we saw HB lifting a huge safe, and now Dad easily bests the brute with a headlock maneuver. So THAT'S how strong Dad is. Then, much later,
Dad gets Worfed by Jack and then Jack gets Worfed by /blocks tvtropes.org again/.

It seems there are some unopened BIRTHDAY PRESENTS which DAD didn't get around to giving you yet.

> John: Present time! Open a present see what's inside!

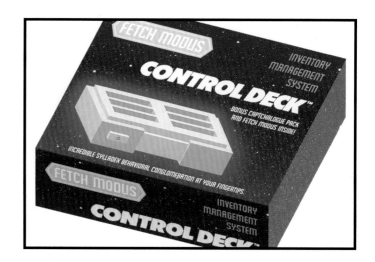

The one on the right seems promising.

You open it to see what is inside and oh god yes.

> John: Obtain SW33TL00T.

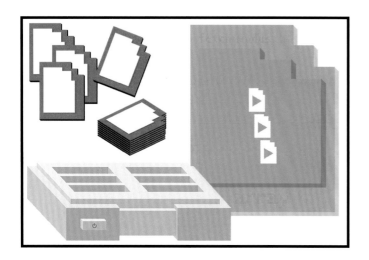

You tear into this thing and put a mean peep on the sw33tloot.

In addition to the MODUS CONTROL DECK, you got a bonus ARRAY FETCH MODUS. Plus another 12 cards, which are practically worthless by this point, but hey you'll take 'em.

It must be great to be a kid in Homestuckworld. Instead of getting Nintendos and stuff for your birthday, you just accumulate more weird and stupid ways to pick stuff up.

First thing you do is flush the
extra cards into your deck.

Ok really this is just way too many cards.

> John: Equip array fetch modus.

The ARRAY MODUS allows you to store and
retrieve any item from any card at any
time. It seems exceptionally serviceable,
albeit difficult to weaponize.

BOOOOOOOORING.

> John: Read instructions for control deck.

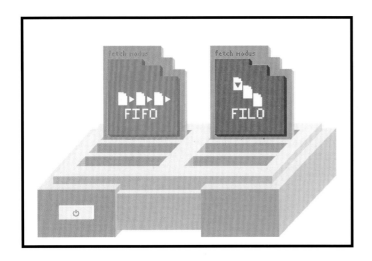

There's nothing to read, really. You just pop
some MODUS CARTRIDGES in the slots, fire it
up, and see what happens.

You start by putting the STACK and QUEUE MODI
in the slots.

John: Even better, skip ahead a few thousand pages to the part of the story where sylladexes don't matter anymore.

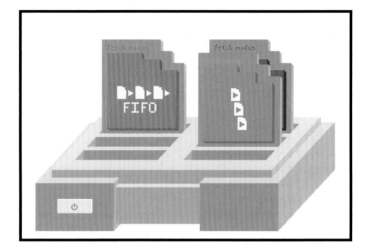

Your sylladex now behaves like both a STACK
and a QUEUE. Items can be removed from either
the top card or the bottom card.

You see no reason at all not to jam the ARRAY
CARTRIDGE in there too. You make sure to blow the
dust out first of course.

The sylladex reconfigures itself into an ARRAY of
distinct QUEUESTACKS.

Now we're talking. This is just the sort of needless
complexity you have come to expect from your
INVENTORY MANAGEMENT SYSTEM.

> John: Unwrap the smallest present first.

I bet most current readers of *Homestuck* aren't even old enough to remember having to blow dust out of game cartridges. Let me tell you, youngsters, life was gritty back then. You had to WORK to play your shitty games. You could be plowing through some dungeon in *Zelda*, and stomp a little too hard on the floor and RESET the whole fuckin' NES. Many of my generation were tormented by that little blinking red light next to the power button which seemed to say, "Ha ha, you were born into an era JUST SLIGHTLY before technology stopped totally sucking."

You have a staunch policy of always saving
the biggest present for last.

ALWAYS.

You receive a box of delicious FRUIT GUSHERS.

Could this birthday get any better?
You don't think so.

> John: Open the big one.

You thought wrong.

> John: Fill up an entire queuestack with
shoes.

Ok, awesome. Queuestack full'a shoes.

> John: Captchalogue Fruit Gushers.

Dang! You spaced out and put it in the wrong queuestack. Don't worry, you'll get the hang of this thing.

> John: Closely inspect Fruit Gushers box.

So delicious. You can't wait to captchalogue one of these packs and make like a million gushers. Screw all this building nonsense! You'd rather make candy.

Wait a minute...

It...

It can't be...

The best thing about this revelation is that when I first included Gushers in HS as a gag, I actually had no idea Betty Crocker made them. It was as mindblowing to me as it was to John.

THE HEINOUS BATTERWITCH HAS HER GNARLED CLAWS IN EVERYTHING.

What do Gushers have to do with baked goods anyway??

How does this make sense???

Why????

WHYYYYYYYYYYYYYYYYYY???????????

>[S] John: Mental breakdown.

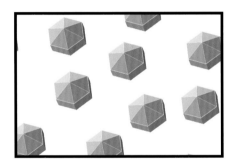

MIXED BERRY SOCIAL ANXIETY DISORDER was discontinued as a flavor. But only because the Condesce ran out of that kind of troll blood.

>[S] Jade: Retrieve package.

Another most unfortunate juxtaposition between bukkake and slime from *Ghostbusters*, a correlation which once again sails right over John's head. Literally, in this case. Also let's take note of "RANCH DRESSING RAMPAGE," which is partially covered. Let's take note of it because it's the funniest one.

Jade: Seriously, just walk over there and pick up the present. Bec won't mind. He's a good dog.

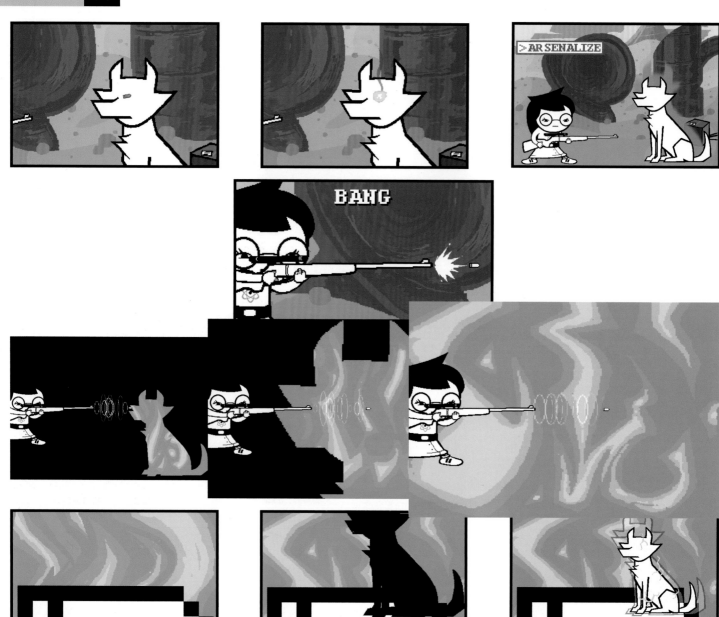

What you don't see in this series of freeze frames is that when Bec appears, for a split second you can see the green sun. This is some very far in advance, blink-of-an-eye foreshadowing. Back when I made this strife page, I did envision a vast, supernatural green sun as the energy source for Bec, and for all First Guardians. But that was well before it picked up steam as a major plot element.

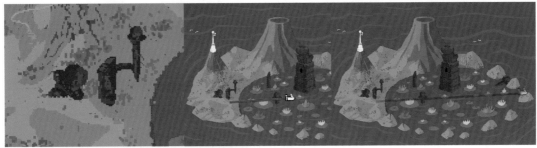

Bec's magic powers were a great excuse to show off Flash's COOL MASKING EFFECTS. Let's be honest here. Showing Bec's expanding and contracting shape clipped out against the area of the new location he's warping to makes the idea of teleportation WAY MORE FUN. Though if we're totally keeping it real it should be noted that this effect is SOMEWHAT LESS COOL ON PAPER.

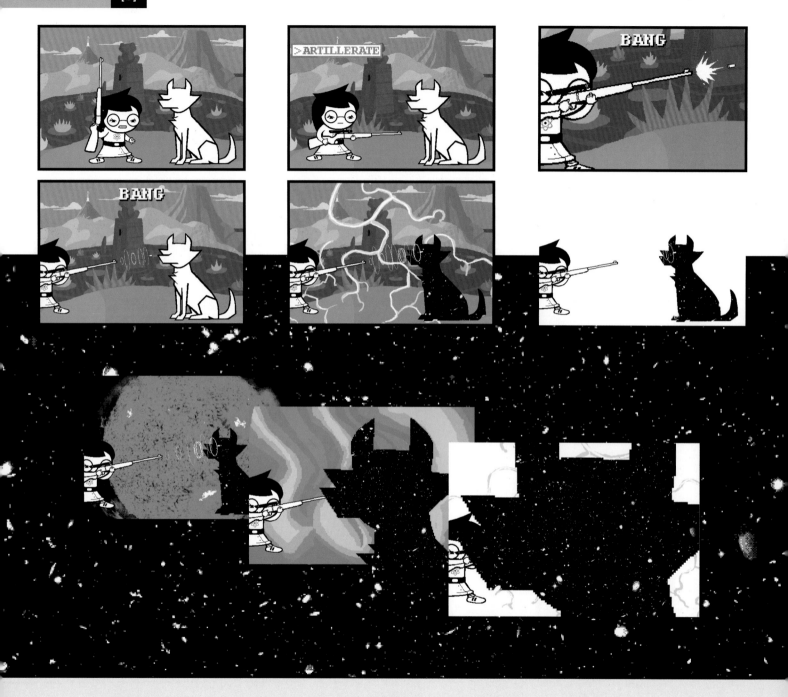

Wait, there it is! Another split-second shot of the sun I mentioned earlier. See? I wasn't lying. But, full disclosure, literally all of my other notes have been lies.

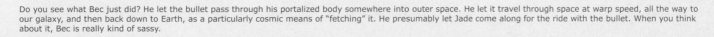

Do you see what Bec just did? He let the bullet pass through his portalized body somewhere into outer space. He let it travel through space at warp speed, all the way to our galaxy, and then back down to Earth, as a particularly cosmic means of "fetching" it. He presumably let Jade come along for the ride with the bullet. When you think about it, Bec is really kind of sassy.

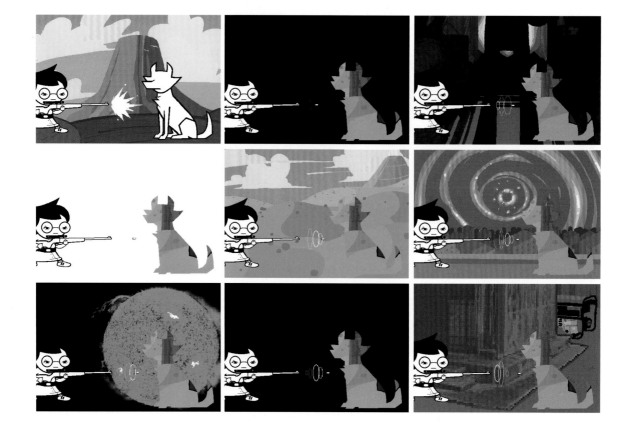

Oh, here's yet another shot of the green sun. Now I just seem silly for saying you couldn't see it a few pages ago. And there's a big red sun appearing one frame before. With a big swirl in it. I wonder if red and green and swirls ever become significant later. Naw.

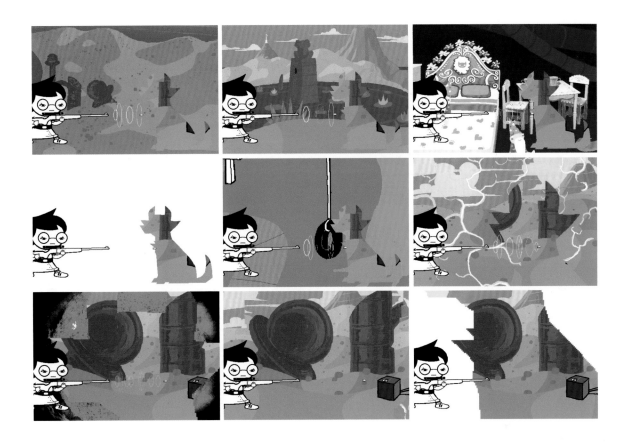

Bec also comes off as a little dickish by implication when you consider he could teleport Jade off the island at any time to go hang out with her friends, or even, you know, lead a normal life somewhere. Then again, he is rather protective and territorial. He doesn't want anyone else horning in on his Jade time.

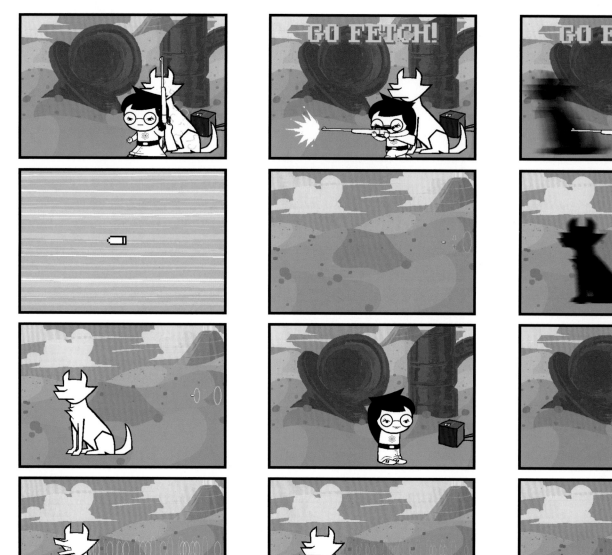

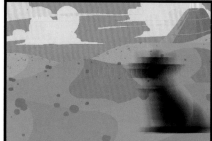

There's a variation on this game that's played with a flashlight instead of a rifle, and Bec fetches the photons.

Jade: Take dog out behind woodshed and give him a big hug. The woodshed is actually an ancient stone monument, though. Yes, just like that. That's fine.

> Rose: Check self for any mixed atoms with cat.

Jade was acting too happy so Vriska put a stop to that. You don't know what I'm talking about if you don't know who Vriska is. Maybe it's better that way.

Nope, no mixed atoms. Looks like you and the kitty
kept your genes to yourselves.

Your new kitty whose name is...

You'll think of one later.

Hey where the heck are you anyway?

> Rose: Look around room.

Oh, you're back home. The well-stocked bar and the
vantage from the window tells you this is your MOM'S
room. Or at least what you thought was her room.

You decide not to be especially melodramatic about
this revelation.

> Rose: Watch the meteor impact.

Huh, that's funny. Shouldn't that place be
unestablished by now?

The downpour of smaller meteors has stopped...

Rose: Peel printed liquor bottle pattern off of shelf surface.

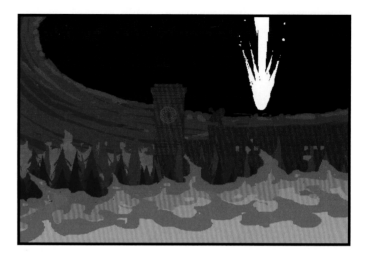

Better get out of here. This room is a powder-keg with all this booze lying around.

> John: Get down to business.

Rose: This is all very stressful. Develop drinking problem later in canon.

Suddenly you are feeling very businessmanlike for some reason.

You just punched a shitload of cards in anticipation of making a whole lot of cool stuff. This time you didn't foolishly destroy any items. You just looked at the codes for some objects you rounded up, and punched them on blank cards.

You wonder how much alchemizing you can get away with before Rose gets back? As if she's got any right to tell you what to do with your hard earned grist. You're the one running around here putting your ass on the line. All she's got to do is mess around with her computer!

Anyway, you better hurry.

> Jade: Dream.

The irony is that Rose is not just messing around with her computer but is now actually in peril. Now that I've explained that for you to understand, let's reflect on how great the word "businessmanlike" is.

You are now dreaming.

Your DREAMBOT is awake and active.

> Jade: Obliquely foreshadow future through interpretive dance

Your silly dance foreshadows nothing and is essentially meaningless.

But it sure is a lot of fun.

> Jade: Quick! Get into bed!

Jade's interpretive dance is literally the only thing in *Homestuck* that foreshadows nothing whatsoever. (Unlike the mysterious arm in the lower left corner, which... Yeah, I'm not even gonna touch that topic in this book.)

You climb into bed and try to get comfortable. But some sort of invisible force is pressing down on you, a strange feeling of cold heavy metal.

This happens every time you try to get into bed! No wonder you can never get any sleep.

> Jade: Realize you can fly!

There is not much to realize.

Of course you can fly.

> Jade: Open the Package.

There is much to speculate about with Jade's dreambot. Did Grandpa Harley build it to record and study Jade's dream life? Or to prevent her from sleepwalking? Dream selves and the rules surrounding them are very significant to the rest of the story. Not only that, but robot bodies become a recurring thing too. What I'm saying is, these are some of the most important pages in HS, if not THE most important.

You stop all this flying around nonsense and examine John's birthday package.

Unfortunately you cannot open it yet! This package has an important journey to make first. You are planning on delivering it momentarily.

Good thing you already know what's inside. Otherwise you would surely be consumed by curiosity and suspense. You sincerely pity anyone who might be forced to endure such a fate.

> Months in the past...

"You sincerely pity anyone who might be forced to endure such a fate" is a rare moment of self-awareness in the story, directed at readers who are, in fact, forced to endure such a fate. I promise it will never happen again.

Enough for the above weather to be seasonably reconcilable...

-- ghostyTrickster [GT] began pestering gardenGnostic [GG] --

GT: hey, happy birthday jade!
GG: yay thank you john!!!!! :D
GT: whew ok, i got your present in the mail JUST on time.
GT: plus i sent rose's and dave's too.
GT: why do your guys'es birthdays got to be all bunched together like that??? you are running me ragged!
GG: heheh i know but it is nice of you to think of us all like that!

See the calendar? There it is. Direct evidence of the other three kids' birth dates. Look how hard John is working to send all his friends gifts wrapped in identical blue packages. He is just flying through the blue wrapping paper.

GT: i can't wait for you to see what i got you. i don't want to spoil it or anything but hopefully it will help you solve those problems you've been having lately.
GT: MYSTERIOUS WINK ;)
GG: im sure it is great, i cant wait either!!!!!
GG: it might take a while to get here from there but it will be worth the wait!
GT: oh man.
GT: i am such an idiot, i forgot about how long it takes you to get stuff.
GT: ARGH.
GG: john thats ok really! im sure will get to me exactly when it needs to and it will be a nice surprise when it does!
GT: ok well i hope so.
GG: <3......
GG: uhhhh hold on
GG: ok im back sorry
GG: i had to tell someone to go away!
GT: oh god.
GT: the trolls again?
GG: yup :o
GT: they have been such a pain in the ass lately.
GT: it seems like there are so many.
GT: there are either like fifty of these retards or it's one guy with a lot of alt accounts.
GG: ive never had any sort of feeling about them or what they want which is kind of weird!!!
GG: but it seems to me like they are probably all different people and not one guy
GG: i have counted twelve
GT: what do they want with us!!!
GG: some people just like to needle others for some reason john
GG: it is like a game i guess. they are like pranksters!!
GT: oh hell no, shittiest pranksters ever.
GG: but i think they are mostly harmless
GG: every so often they manage to get through my block filter and hassle me. its been going on for years! actually some of them are kind of funny i think hehe
GT: oh wow, what? years??
GT: ok, well i am sick of them.
GT: i've been thinking of changing my pesterchum handle to throw them off the trail.
GT: so...
GT: i guess i'm gonna do that.

> John: Make totems.

This is a very simple conversation, but there's so much going on here. First of all, Jade is being a filthy liar again. She knows what's in that box. Second, the casual allusion to "too many trolls" makes you wonder which ones are hassling her. Bet you she's been getting HAMMERED by Gamzee. Third, John calls them "retards," which is pretty ableist of him. Who knew a thirteen-year-old kid could be such a jerk? And finally, we learn why he switched from GT to EB. Whew, that's a lot. With this kind of economical dialogue, there's no WAY this story will turn out to be more than half a million words.

You have already carved a few TOTEMS, but you have had to return to the living room for more CRUXITE DOWELS. Your carving work is not nearly complete.

Every time you reenter your room, you shudder at the recent handiwork of some mischievous imps. You just can't turn your back on them for a second!

Rotten imps. Those posters were like children to you.

> Rose: Flee room.

At long last, you have returned to your bedroom with a stable power supply and internet connection.

VODKA MUTINI purrs at your side.

You SUPPOSE you will call it Mutie for short.

> Rose: Pester John.

And so begins the tradition of naming pets stupid things, and then renaming them to other stupid things later on at least once, before they are eventually slain.

TT: That's quite a totem collection.
TT: What are you planning?
EB: oh whoa hi!
EB: oh...
EB: gonna make some stuff.
EB: are you ok? hasn't your house been on fire for like...
EB: five hours now?
TT: No, that was the nearby forest, which up until quite recently would have been best described as "on fire".
TT: But you may be excited to learn that just as recently, my house finally notched that achievement.
EB: wow, congrats i guess?
TT: Thank you. Have you seen Dave?
EB: nah.
EB: his bro is probably busy kicking his ass.
EB: that's probably all there is to say on the matter.
TT: Ok.
TT: I'm going to start putting this grist to use too.
TT: Let's be sparing with the frivolous knickknack breeding and focus on getting you up to the gate, ok?
EB: yeah, ok i hear you, but...
EB: i think we'll have plenty. i've been killing imps all over the house and now its lousy with gushers.
TT: Gushers?
EB: i mean grist.
EB: serves them right for ruining my posters. the bastards.
TT: Which posters?
EB: don't you see? my sweet movie posters. look at them, they're fucking ruined.
TT: John.
EB: ??????
TT: Are you suggesting that imps are responsible for defacing your movie posters?
EB: uh, YEAH?
TT: Your posters have looked like that ever since I first saw your room.
TT: The moment we started playing this game.
TT: I thought you had defaced them ironically to mock your father's interests.
TT: John?
TT: ...?
EB: VERY FUNNY ROSE HAHAHAHAHAHAHAHAHAHAHAHA

Rose should be really excited to learn of John's mental illness, because of her interest in psychology. Too bad she doesn't actually know what she's talking about, since she's thirteen, and you have to go to college for that.

EB: NICE JOKE
EB: GREAT JOKE THERE ROSE
EB: TOP OF THE LINE PRANK
EB: HE HE
EB: HA HA HA HA HA
TT: This is good.
TT: Laughter is probably the best way to avoid being especially melodramatic about the revelation.
EB: yes
EB: YES
EB: LET'S KEEP THIS JOKE GOING
EB: BECAUSE IT IS SUCH A GOOD ONE
EB: HA HA HA HA
EB: OH MY
EB: HA HA HA HA HA HA
EB: HA HA HA HA HA HA HA HA HA HA HA HA HA HA HA HA HA HA

Gamzee sure did a number on that poor kid's head. Fuckin' chucklevoodoos.

> WV: Descend.

You cannot descend from the top of your mobile station. The loose cable you gathered up and tied together is not yet long enough to allow you to reach the ground safely.

You have used all the cable you can find. You will have to come up with another plan.

> WV: Sacrifice your MAYORAL SASH for more CABLES.

WV: Go limp, fall to ground headfirst. Use pumpkin bindle as protective headgear.

ABSOLUTELY NOT WHAT ARE YOU CRAZY

A MAYOR DOES NOT RELINQUISH HIS MAYORAL SASH
UNDER ANY CIRCUMSTANCES EVER PERIOD

> WV: Appearify the temple.

That's such a dumb idea. Not as dumb as using your
sash, but it comes close. That temple is way too
big. You'd probably just end up appearifying
a chunk of useless boring rock.

Wait, what's that?

There's something dangling from the top of one of
the towers near the temple.

> WV: Command Serenity to carry the rope
to you.

WV: Measure mayoral sash with yardstick. WV: Put top hat and monocle in bindle. WV: Wonder why top hat and monocle aren't real. AH: Draw all these bonus panels
and make book longer. No wait don't.

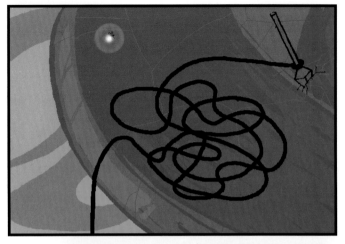

She is a tiny insect and cannot possibly lift more than the weight of a pumpkin seed!!!

She does however inform you of what the ledge contains through a series of informative blinks. There is an old rusty HARPOON lodged into the crumbling rock. Tied to it is a bunched-up jumble of HANDY CABLE. This strikes you as convenient! It is almost as if someone knew you would need a bunch of cable, and that you would have a MAYORAL SASH made out of cable, and that you were particularly attached to that MAYORAL SASH and would stubbornly refuse to use it.

Anyone who knew that much would surely possess a special gift! Alas it seems a bit far fetched.

> WV: Get ye rope.

Ok, we just established it was a cable and not a rope, but that's ok.

You take a hasty swig from one of your DELICIOUS PAWNS and put it down.

You then quickly adjust the coordinates to appearify the jumble of HANDY CABLE.

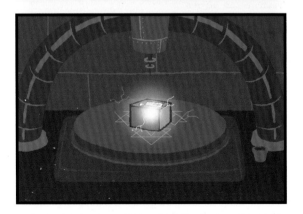

Uh...

Jade saw WV in a dream and said well OBVIOUSLY he's not going to part with that sweet sash. Better bunch up some spare cable here to use as bait.

Oh, of course. The time wasn't set to the present moment. Somehow it got reset to a few hundred years ago.

It is some sort of present from the past... in the present.

Attached is an envelope. It looks extremely important.

You open the envelope. Inside is a letter and another envelope.

This is all highly confusing and you do not know what to make of it.

Still it is obviously critical MAYORAL BUSINESS which you take very seriously and you will defend this package with your life.

> WV: Try to appearify the cable again.

WV: Look at letter. But we don't get to see the letter yet, not for a while, okay good, stuff like that always happens. What, do you think storytellers just come right out and SHOW you things? lol

167

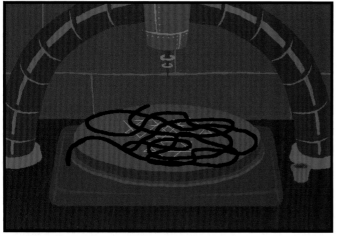

You set the time to the present, and appearify the
JUMBLE OF CABLE.

> WV: Take obvious course of action.

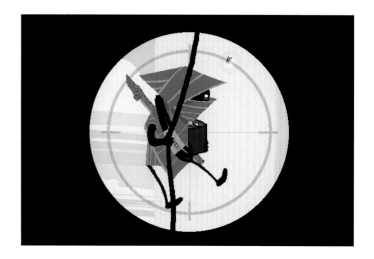

You tie all the cable together and carefully
lower your precious **PUMPKIN BINDLE**.

You then rappel down the station with the
PACKAGE, which must not leave your side.

Which is to say, THE PRESENT MOMENT PRECISELY...

> Years in the future...

WV: You forgot the little flower pot.

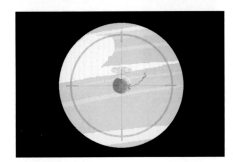

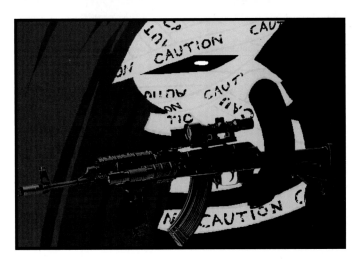

An AIMLESS RENEGADE prepares for company.

> Rose: Build as much as you can as fast as you can.

LADY GAGA??? Oh, no. It's a black carapace man with a machine gun. Trivia: it's the same machine gun last boss has. AR isn't last boss though. He's not really last boss material.

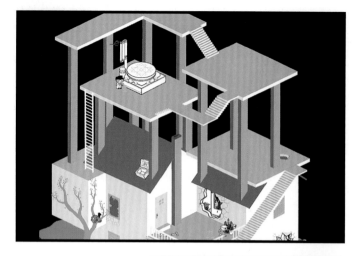

EB: ok, while i make some stuff here
can you keep an eye out for imps?
EB: just keep the safe or tub handy or
something.
EB: it'll serve them right for trashing
my posters.
TT: I keep telling you the posters were
always like that.
EB: AND I KEEP TELLING YOU HA HA VERY
FUNNY
TT: Here, look.
TT: http://tinyurl.com/0413nanna
TT: http://tinyurl.com/0413weirdo

Sprite prototyped once more with grandmother's remains. She treats John to some helpful exposition in a friendly and maternal (grandmaternal?) manner.

Co-player has displayed inexplicably capricious behavior since arrival. Stress-related? Contracted virus indigenous to realm? It should be noted he was kind of a weird guy anyway.

EB: yeah, i saw those, but...
EB: they didn't look like that before. you must have changed them.
TT: Even if I had the motive for such a bizarre and pointless deception, where would I find
the time?
TT: I don't even have Photoshop.
EB: then why didn't you TELL me they were there???
TT: I had no reason to think you were not aware of them.
TT: I thought they were strange, certainly, but was not struck by any particular impulse to
discuss them.
EB: ok, it still doesn't make sense though.
EB: implying that i drew them a while ago and then forgot and couldn't see them and now
suddenly see them.
EB: that's stupid, what would that even mean.

In the grand scheme of things, I wonder which will stop working first: these tinyurl links or mspaintadventures.com itself?

TT: It looks like you were in your father's room recently.
EB: yeah.
TT: And how did it make you feel to discover what was in there?
EB: oh no, i just realized!
EB: you are going to psycho-therapify me.
EB: well don't bother!
TT: Maybe I am just being a friend?
EB: maybe...
EB: /EYES SUSPSICIOSLY
EB: anyway i guess you saw what's in there, it's boring and there's not much to even see.
TT: That doesn't matter.
TT: What matters is how seeing it affected you.
TT: I think it clearly has in some way.
EB: well...
EB: i don't know, at first i was nervous to go in and find more of his weird clowns, because of course they are stupid and i hate them a lot.
EB: but then when i didn't see any, it was weird.
EB: i felt weirdly, like... disappointed almost.
TT: Is it fair to say this changed your perception of your father?
EB: yeah, i guess.
TT: Is it such a stretch to conclude it changed your perception of other things as well?
EB: uh no, maybe not.
EB: but what are you getting at?
EB: it sounds like you're saying i'm crazy!

> John: Alchemize.

ARE YOUR SHIPPING FIRES STOKED YET? Let's face it, this is a bland ship. The first boy and girl introduced in the story? Please. Buying into this ship is kind of jumping the gun. Like when a shareholder sells off stock at the first sign of trouble. John x Rose is a ship for the nervous investor.

TT: I don't like to use the word "crazy".
EB: oh god.
EB: see?? this is therapy bullshit!
TT: That was a joke.
TT: But anyway, whether it means you are crazy or not, consider this theory:
TT: Your presumably longstanding tendency for scrawling this imagery is really your subconsious trying to express something disturbing within you.

TT: Possibly something from your past, which you have blocked out.
TT: And since you have suppressed it, your conscious self cannot acknowledge the drawings, therefore they have been invisible until now.
EB: why now?
TT: Perhaps because you have seen evidence that conflicts with the worldview your subconscious has constructed to obfuscate the truth.
TT: That your dad is not necessarily the clown-loving maniac you thought he was.
TT: All along, this negative attribute buried in your psyche may have been projected on to him, and subsequently reviled, as a sort of defense mechanism.
EB: but this is absurd, my dad LOVES these shitty clowns.
EB: he's got all these statues and paintings EVERYWHERE.
TT: Is it unthinkable that over the years it was he who believed you were the one with a passion for clowns? Because of the all the strange drawings in your room?
TT: A father then embraces a son's hobby to establish a stronger bond.
TT: Or wages a campaign of passive-aggresive mockery of your interests.
TT: Either is plausible. I don't know your dad that well.
EB: i dunno.
EB: not sure about all this.
EB: but i think we need to stop and acknowledge the bunny sassacre fedora i just made.
TT: It's awesome.
EB: yeah.

It's not that awesome.

EB: wow, what are you doing by the way?
EB: rose, sorry to say but this is all looking kind of silly!
TT: I'm trying to spread the upward construction around so there is a more substantial foundation for later on.
TT: But I'm starting to wonder if it will be strong enough.
TT: It's kind of starting to wobble a little.
TT: I don't think brick chimneys were meant to serve this architectural purpose.
EB: yeah no shit!
TT: I might have to adopt a different building strategy.
TT: Stick to more load-bearing walls, and blockier shapes, especially since grist has been easier to come by lately.
EB: ok, but you really must be running low on time by now, right?
TT: Right.
EB: STRIIIIIIDEEEERRRRRRR!!!!!

>[S] Jade: Dream up extra arms and play advanced bass solo.

Chimneystuck, starring Rose Lalonde. She wins. Everyone else go home.

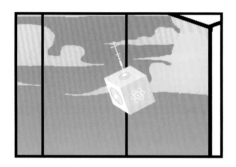

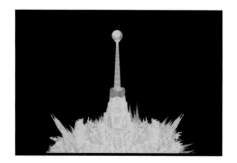
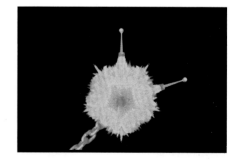

Existence of Prospit revealed. This is another one of those incremental pages that broaden the scope and scale of the story. It doesn't stop from keeping to happen. Who really knows what the gravitational pull of the planet is or if it's strong enough to keep the moon in orbit. Hence the chain. Alternatively, it's just a cool thing for a golden fantasy planet to have.

> Jade: Change wardrobifier to cycle thru STAR HEART HORSESHOE

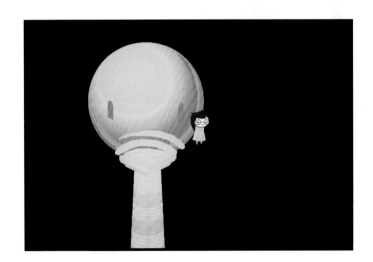

Ok, good idea.

You leave the MOON in the cycle
though cause you like it.

> Jade: Go explore the golden city.

Prospit and Derse are made from collaging dozens of cathedral bits and heavily processing them in Photoshop. There's a lot of collaging in HS, but the most intensive examples probably appear in these settings. They are revisited quite a lot throughout the story. What I am saying is, I have googled more than my share of cathedrals. Way more than you have.

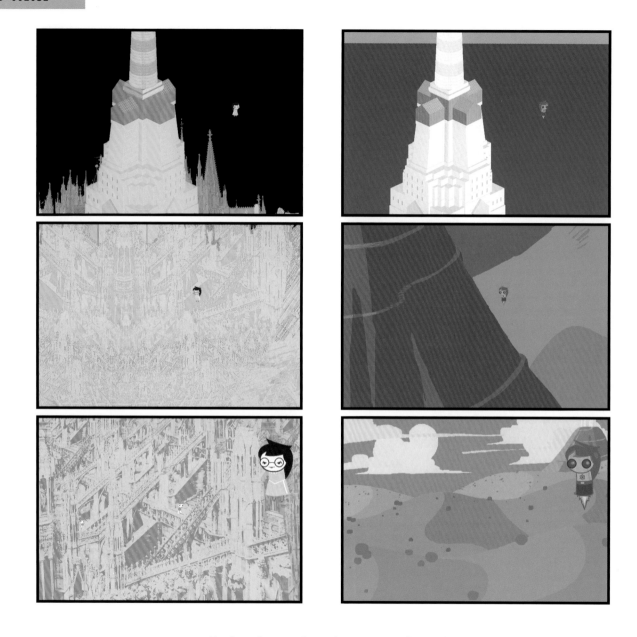

> Jade: Go and make a new friend.

The bot goes where she goes. If you're Bec, it's probably funny to be hanging out on the island and to frequently see this little robo girl floating around as if she's got important stuff to do, talking to thin air and such. Then again, it's probably not that funny to him, since he's a dog.

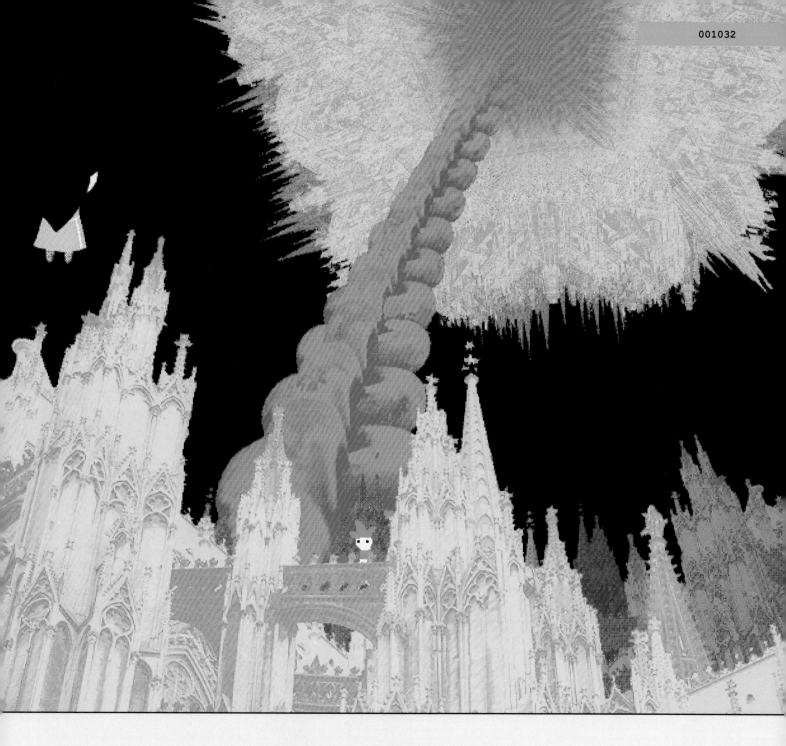

Jade: Compliment tiny crude drawing of Prospitian on lovely hat.

PM: Be recognized as PM by reader. Reader: Ohhhhhh.

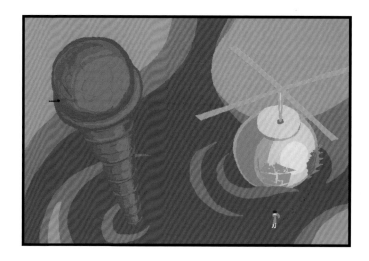

> WV: Eat letter and envelope.

Will you cut that out! You have company.

> WV: Look behind you!

He's confused, because they're deliciously green, but only partially green. So this is the best idea he has. Maybe he doesn't understand the concept of licking?

See? Over there.

> WV: Read letter.

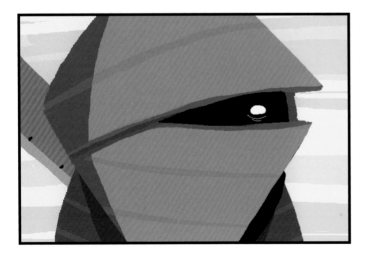

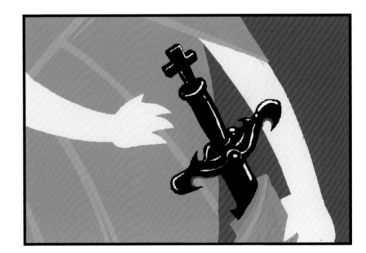

Jade is obviously just setting them up on a date. She is shipping them, through the literal shipping of a parcel. How ironic. Who am I kidding, I burned through all my irony credits an act and a half ago.

The Aimless Renegade sure has bad aim. Almost like he's an...

Unreliable...

Marksman.

> WV: Give present! Hooray!!!

What is the worm doing with the mailbox? It probably thinks it's helping. Why is everyone being so cute STOP IT YOU ARE UNDER ATTACK.

> Jade: Gracefully fly to the other golden tower.

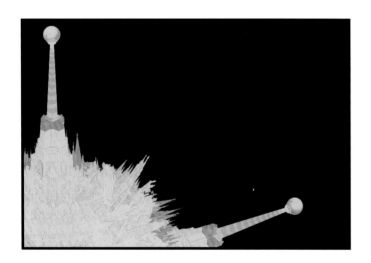
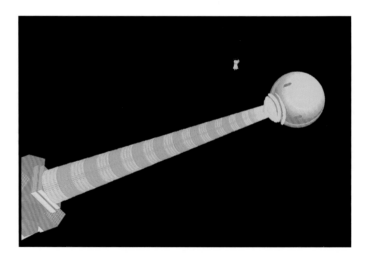

You decide to check on your neighbor.

> Jade: Inspect neighbor's tower.

You fail to fly gracefully. You fly like a silly doofus instead.

It is very much the same as your own! The only difference is that
this one is home to a young boy instead of a young girl.

You peer through the window.

John is of course sound asleep. It looks like
he is having troubled dreams as usual.

You cannot disturb his slumber though.
He will wake up when he is ready!

Speaking of John, you wonder if he got the
birthday present you sent him? Or for that matter,
if you even remembered to send it?

Darn! You get so confused sometimes. If only you had
some system in place to help you remember things.

Jade's dreaming confusion and forgetfulness is kind of an odd symptom that's never quite duplicated by another waking dream self. There are two possibilities. One is, I was still ironing out the dream self rules early in the story and that symptom never developed in others. Or two, because her sleeping habits are imposed on her unnaturally by external forces. GUESS WHICH EXPLANATION I PREFER.

Your MOON is getting very close to SKAIA. You had better go inside soon. It is never a very good idea to be outside during the ECLIPSE.

Maybe you can take the opportunity to log onto your computer and ask John about his present. You just know he will think it is awesome, and it will be a great way to thank him for the wonderful present he got you!

> John: Alchemize in a 1980's time-lapse montage.

That would be pretty cool, and would promote the appearance to the audience that a whole lot was getting done in not much time, but it also sounds like kind of a pain in the ass so you decide to play it straightup this time.

Rose has moved the ALCHEMITER back down to the deck while she reworks the building project up there. Just as well because it will save you a lot of legwork. Between this thing, the designix and the lathe, that's a whole lot of scrambling around!

> John: Recombine hammer and pogo ride.

Sburb tip: you only earn the ability to do 1980s time-lapse montages after you go god tier.

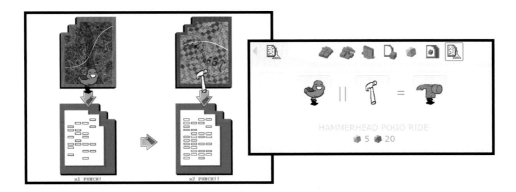

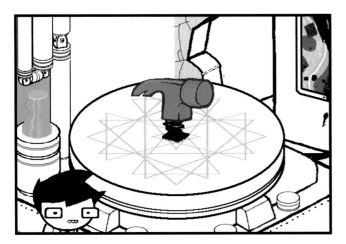

This time instead of overlapping (&&) the two cards which created the POGO HAMMER, you use the two codes to double-punch (||) a blank card, producing a different hole pattern.

The result is the HAMMERHEAD POGO RIDE. It doesn't look like it's as much fun as the original ride, but to be fair it's probably a lot safer.

Double-punching cards creates patterns with more holes, rather than less holes by overlapping cards. This strikes you as a viable method for combining more than two items without whittling down to too few holes, or too many! Just mix up the overlaps and double-punches, and the sky's the limit.

> John: Combine ghost shirt and suit.

You make the GREEN SLIME GHOST SUIT.

Pretty swanky, but you are not completely satisfied with the wardrobe upgrade yet.

> John: Combine ghost suit and Wise Guy book.

You make the WISE GUY SLIME SUIT.

This is so much better. It seems there are lots of secret trickstery gimmicks concealed in OH SHIT THERE GO THE CARDS

> John: Combine glasses and PDA.

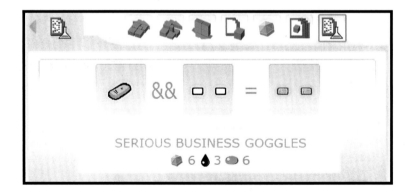

The first official *Homestuck* "alchemy binge." It is the funnest thing that can possibly happen in HS. It is literally all downhill from here.

You make the SERIOUS BUSINESS GOGGLES.

This is a pretty nice hands-free communication solution, and it makes you look way cooler, like one of the kids from SPY KIDS or something.

God that was a good movie.

REAL SPIES...only smaller

> John: Combine sledgehammer, telescope, and Sassacre text.

You make the TELESCOPIC SASSACRUSHER, at pretty considerable expense. This thing could probably pound an ogre into crudeburger.

Of course you have no hope of lifting it whatsoever.

> John: Combine gushers and blue ectoplasm.

If you ask me, there aren't enough hammers with handles that are fully functional, presumably delicate telescopes. Not enough hammers made out of huge, ancient joke books either.

HELLACIOUS BLUE PHLEGM ANEURYSM GUSHERS

🗇 24 🔵 30 💿 18

You mix your Gushers with some of the blue slime Nanna left on the wall to make a box of HELLACIOUS BLUE PHLEGM ANEURYSM GUSHERS (WITH GHOSTLY HEALING PROPERTIES!)

THESE SHOULD BE CONVENIENT, IF SOMEWHAT UNAPPETIZING.

> John: Combine fake arm, blue ectoplasm, and PDA.

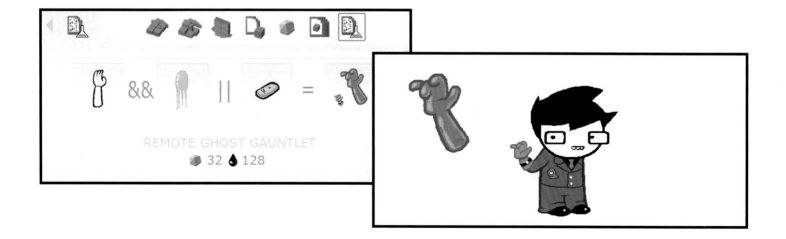

REMOTE GHOST GAUNTLET

🟦 32 💧 128

A blue phlegm aneurysm is one of the least pleasant aneurysms you can have. If you ask a neuroscientist about it, they won't say anything but will just give you a knowing look of dismay.

You make the REMOTE GHOST GAUNTLET.

It looks like when you put on the special computer-glove it lets you control the big slimy ghost hand.

The GHOST GAUNTLET appears to have a considerably higher lift capacity than your own puny arms.

> John: Combine ghost gauntlet and bathroom mirror.

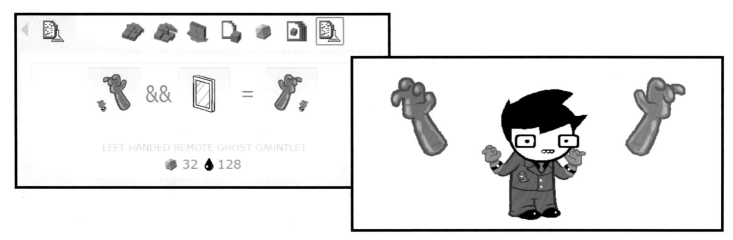

LEFT HANDED REMOTE GHOST GAUNTLET

32 128

You make a LEFT HANDED REMOTE GHOST GAUNTLET to complete the pair.

BECAUSE YOU DON'T SEE WHY THE HELL NOT.

> John: Combine umbrella and straight razor.

Honestly I forgot until just now that a mirror could be combined with items to flip them. I don't think that clever tactic was ever used again. But then, in a universe where sprites can just "flip turn-ways," maybe it's not actually that useful?

You make the BARBER'S BEST FRIEND.

It suddenly seems worthwhile to you to go nab that UMBRELLAKIND
STRIFE SPECIBUS that's been lying in the study for a while.

> John: Combine gushers and shaving cream.

You make a deadly BETTY CROCKER BARBASOL BOMB.

Be careful with that thing! Jesus!!

> John: Combine Ghost Dad poster with...

The Batterwitch produces these things en masse for third-world armies. A more heartless profiteer from war and suffering you will never find.

192

Ok, you have a cool idea for something to do with your GHOST DAD POSTER, but it looks like you drew shit all over that one too without realizing it.

Lousy goddamn stupid subconscious!

Anyway, you think you have an idea how to clean it up.

> John: Captchalogue/punch Heath Ledger Joker figurine.

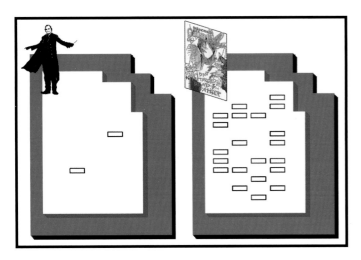

If you can somehow "subtract" the code of the JOKER FIGURINE from the code of the poster, it might work.

Luckily, the Joker code only has two holes, making the task very simple. The defaced Cosby poster shares those holes. You determine that the defaced Cosby could only result from a double-punching with the Joker, if your theory is correct. This means the original Cosby poster had one of those holes punched, or the other, or neither, making three total possibilities.

You try out all three possible codes, yielding:

- 1 POTTED PLANT
- 1 PAINTING OF A HORSE ATTACKING A FOOTBALL PLAYER
- 1 CLEAN COSBY POSTER

SUCCESS.

> John: Combine Cosby poster with computer.

You didn't follow any of that. BTW I own that horse painting IRL. 'Nuff said.

You make the COSBYTOP COMPUTER.

This thing is probably a useless piece of shit, but making it
has caused you to feel an alarming sense of satisfaction.

> John: Combine Dad's hat and Problem Sleuth game.

You make another ordinary FEDORA with FOUR PIECES OF CANDY CORN inside.

> John: Combine Hammer and Problem Sleuth game.

Bill Cosby is the perfect father. We all know this. Whereas Bing Crosby, though quite fatherly onscreen, was actually a total douche to his real kids. I didn't know this until way after I put him in HS. I wonder if Dad would have a dramatic breakdown if he learned that?

*YEARS LATER EDIT — HA HA, LET'S POLITELY SIDESTEP THE FACT THAT HE'S NOW BETTER KNOWN AS A SERIAL RAPIST THAN A GOOD FATHER. HA HA, WHAT SEX CRIMES SPANNING FIVE DECADES??? HA HA, WOW, MOVING ON!

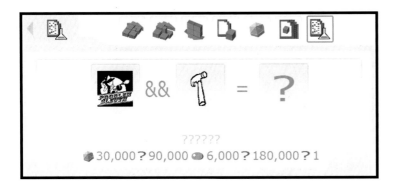

Whatever this item is, you cannot make it yet! It requires a ludicrous amount of grist, some types of which you have not even encountered.

> John: Combine iron and pogo hammer.

You make the WRINKLEFUCKER.

I don't think we ever got any more clues to what the *Problem Sleuth* hammer was. Probably just a Sepulchritude-themed hammer or something. Whatever it was, even though it seems powerful by its cost right now, other weapons later surely left it in the dust.

*But for real, re: the Cosby debacle. Given that I was just saying what a douche Bing Crosby was, it makes sense that Bill Cosby turned out to be one as well. These two figures are cosmically linked in the *Homestuck* mythos, which has eternally bound their souls together whether they like it or not. Both iconic father figures. Both wretched human beings. The circle of depravity is complete.

195

So much sweet loot. You'd almost think it was simultaneously your birthday, AND Christmas or something.

Of course you know that is ridiculous and could never conceivably happen.

>[S] Dave: Strife!

This page was posted on the site on Christmas. The moment took place on John's birthday in the story. With that one joke, it became official. The comic somehow consists more than 100% of fourth-wall-bending dramatic irony.

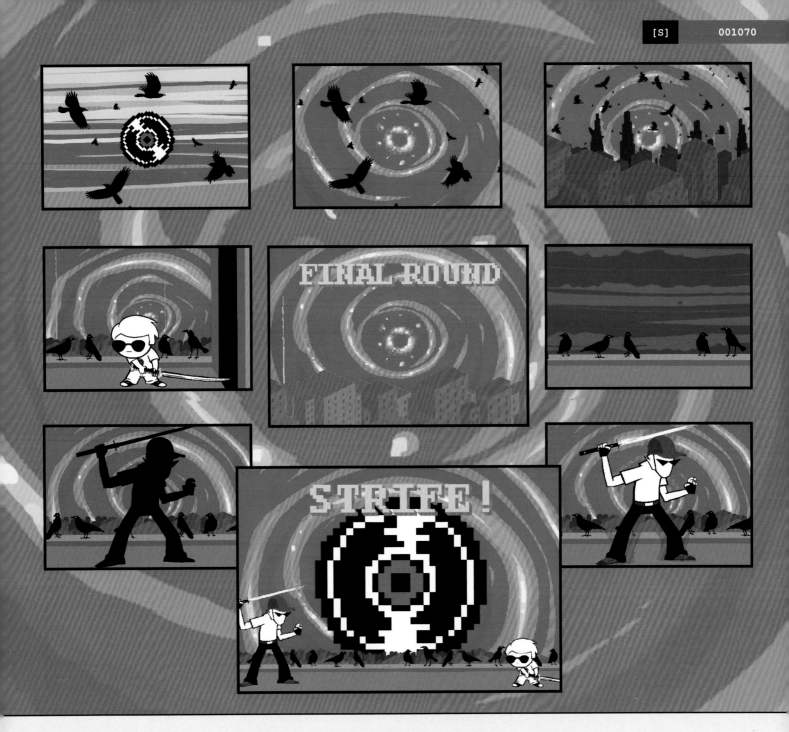

The crows do enjoy a good Strider beatdown. They gather on the roof every day waiting for the lopsided brawl to start. Maybe that's why the crow came through Dave's window squawking at him. It was saying, "Hey, get your ass on the roof so we can watch your bro beat the shit out of you! CAW!!!"

Cal's like, DIS GONNA BE GOOD.

Now the record on Dave's shirt is broken and stays that way forever. Bro has a way of foreshadowing important events in an oblique and violent manner. Like when he stabs the big record plateau later. He couldn't make it any clearer unless he just shouted, "DAVE. YOU'RE SUPPOSED TO SCRATCH A BIG RECORD IN HALF LATER. GET WITH THE PROGRAM."

-- **turntechGodhead [TG] began pestering ectoBiologist [EB]** --

TG: bro just kicked my ass

Well at least that creepy puppet was destroyed, and we'll never have to see him again. Let's put this ugly chapter in *Homestuck* behind us.

TG: thats really all there is to say on the matter

>[S] Jade: Pester John.

You can tell Dave and John are tight bros because he sends him brief updates like this now and then. Nothing fancy. No bigger point to make. Just got his ass kicked, that's all.

```
-- gardenGnostic [GG] began pestering ectoBiologist [EB] at 13:25 --

GG: john did you get my package??
EB: oh hey!
EB: no, not yet.
GG: darn! are you sure? it was in a green box.....
EB: oh!
EB: yes, but it is in my dad's car and he is still out at the store.
EB: he should be back soon.
GG: great!!! so what are you up to today?
EB: i am up to my neck in this sburb stuff.
EB: TT is making a royal mess of my house.
GG: lol!
GG: whats sburb??
EB: oh, it is this game.
EB: it's ok i guess. i'm still figuring it out.
```

Here we see an earlier conversation repeated from Jade's POV, while a fantastical animation is blowing your mind. Except not, because you're reading a book. If your face hurts, that's cause you're frowning too hard right now.

```
GG: whoa what was that?????
EB: what was what?
GG: there was a loud noise outside my house!!
GG: it sounded like an explosion!!!!
EB: wow, really?
GG: i will go outside and look....
EB: oh man, alright but be careful, ok?
GG: i will! :)

 -- gardenGnostic [GG] ceased pestering ectoBiologist [EB] --
```

It's possibly more clear in the animation (???), but everything happening here is a mirage created by Prospit's moon passing through Skaia. The clouds blow through the golden cityscape and project visions, in this case showing Jade's moon tower in place of her house on the island, and then showing what her island looked like millions of years ago when the volcano was active and the ocean wasn't there. At that time, a meteor came through a portal and crashed, making the crater, which is now a lagoon.

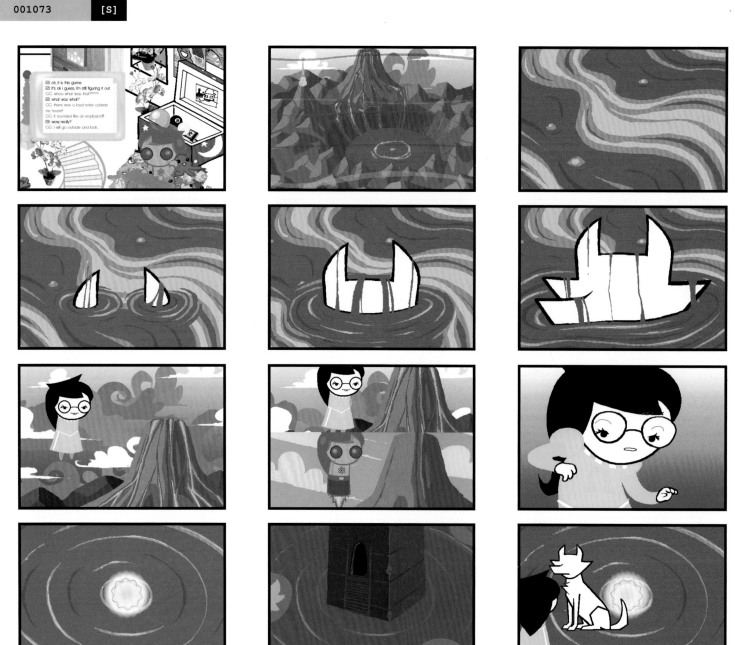

The frog temple spawned from the seed left by the meteor. Inside the temple is a time capsule. The first thing to come out of the capsule was Bec and he just sorta hung out there for eons. HS BONUS TRIVIA QUESTION: Do you know what the last thing out of the capsule is?

-- gardenGnostic [GG] began pestering ectoBiologist [EB] --

GG: im back!
EB: oh hi!
GG: i went to investigate the explosion i heard
EB: was it by any chance a meteor?
GG: yes!!!!!
GG: how did you know??
EB: oh man, it's kind of a long story!
EB: anyway, are you ok? did it blow up your yard or start a fire or anything?
GG: no i am fine!
GG: it landed a pretty good ways from my house and i went to look at it
GG: and its pretty big!
GG: but bec doesnt want me to go near it
GG: so i came home
GG: he seems to think its dangerous!
EB: well gosh, he's probably right!
GG: oh!!!! did you get my package yet? :O
EB: er...
EB: yeah, i was trying to get it, but rose dropped my car into a weird spooky bottomless pit and the package was in the car and im really sorry about that.
GG: oh no!
EB: wow, ok, i guess i should start at the beginning.
EB: see, a meteor blew up my neighborhood.
GG: thats terrible john! im so sorry!
EB: but i'm ok! and my house is too, sort of.

Dream Jade is too spacey to remember that all she has to do is play bullet fetch to get Bec out of the way.

EB: that game i was telling you about, sburb which i was playing with rose, sort of transported me somewhere at the last minute.
EB: but now i'm trapped here and it's weird and dark and i can't find my dad and i just lost the car and my copy of the game in the pit and i think i have to save the world from the apocalypse!!!
GG: O_O
GG: well.....
GG: it sounds really crazy and kind of scary but.....
GG: it also sounds kind of exciting!
GG: i dont know john maybe this is your destiny
GG: if anyone can save the world i think it is probably you!
EB: wow, you think so?
GG: yes!
EB: well ok, BUT.
EB: it's not even that simple!
EB: i was about to connect to rose to help transport her and save her from meteors and fire and stuff.
EB: but she lost battery power and i lost the game disc!
EB: so i think i have to get TG to use his copy to save her!
EB: but that jackass won't shut up and stop rapping and stuff.
GG: hahaha
GG: he is so silly!
EB: yeah. anyway i should talk to him about it, so brb.

What Jade should have said was, "if anyone can save the world i think it is probably you, and 12 trolls, and maybe 4 other kids and like 12 other dead trolls and some chess people and stuff, and maybe not so much the world as all of reality or something!"

Whew, false alarm. Jade and John almost met there and had a fun and heartwarming reunion. Let's buckle in for another few thousand pages of isolation and estrangement, or, as I like to call it, *Homestuck*'s wheelhouse.

```
-- gardenGnostic [GG] began pestering ectoBiologist [EB] --

GG: hey!!!!
EB: whoa, there you are!
GG: how is your adventure going john?
EB: it's ok, i am making some progress, and rose finally connected again so she is helping
me now.
GG: thats good!!
EB: oh but, like...
EB: i don't think i am actually saving the world here. :(
EB: i dunno what i'm really accomplishing but i guess it's not that.
GG: hmm well i think whatever it is it must be pretty important!
GG: dont lose hope john i think it will all turn out for the best if you stay positive....
GG: just keep listening to your grandmothers advice!!!
EB: yeah, you're probably right.
EB: but, um...
EB: i don't think i mentioned nanna to you, did i?
GG: oh uhhh.......
GG: i dont know didnt you???
EB: hmm, i dunno, maybe you talked rose or dave about it or something.
GG: yeah maybe that was it!!
EB: they're really weird when they talk to me about you, like they're always trying convince
me you have some spooky powers, but i'm always like no she seems like a pretty regular girl
to me!
GG: heheheh :D
EB: but then when i think back maybe there are times when it seems like you know some
things?
EB: like maybe you know more about a thing than you are telling me? i dunno.
```

John: Solicit grandmother's advice, cookies.

```
GG: oh well john
GG: i want to explain lots of things to you....
GG: some things that i know
GG: im just......
GG: waiting!
EB: waiting for what!
GG: oh! john!!!
GG: i forgot i was messaging you about that meteor that fell near my house!
EB: oh yeah.
EB: what ever happened with that?
GG: oh boy.... well........
GG: it turns out i was confused about it...
GG: really confused! o_o;
GG: see i guess i fell asleep for a while and.....
GG: lost track of time
GG: that happens!!
EB: yeah i know, tell me about it!
EB: maybe you should like, wear an alarm clock or something.
EB: so what was the deal with the meteor?
GG: well.....
GG: its hard to explain!!!
GG: but...
GG: i know what it is now!
GG: and now i know everythings going to be ok!!!
EB: so what is it???
EB: or is this just another thing you're "waiting" to tell me???
GG: oh gosh john i really want to tell you all this stuff!!!
GG: but i cant yet
GG: i really think you need to wake up first!
EB: huh?
GG: well ok not literally
GG: well ok maybe KINDA literally!!
EB: AUGH!!!!!!!!!!!!!!
EB: stop being so confusing!!!!
GG: lol :)
GG: anyway time for you to go john
GG: i think you have some company!!!
GG: <3
```

> Jade: Update colourful reminders.

I think Jade literally does mean literally. But whatever, she's just a silly kid.

You take a moment to gather your thoughts after your dream. While you are asleep it can get very confusing figuring out what is really happening and what isn't. Especially during the ECLIPSE, when you are exposed to many visions of the past, present, and future through a variety of CLOUD MIRAGES. It is only after you wake up that you are able to start making sense of it all, and your REMINDERS help you do this!

But on reflection, there wasn't much in the dream about the future. You were quite surprised to see your DOG in your dream though. It was the first time the crafty guardian has ever appeared in a dream! You have learned that today is his birthday, just like it is for your other best friend. You have always wondered about this, and never had the chance to throw him a party and bake him a cake. Now you can!

But if you do, it seems that you will need A LOT of candles.

Some of the reminders are to help her keep track of which DeviantArt accounts her furry posters are from.

Bec has never allowed you to enter the MYSTIC RUINS for reasons you never understood. You always assumed it was on account of your protection. But your dream has strongly suggested to you that is where you need to go now!

Since your DREAMBOT is secured in its chamber and does not need to be looked after, Bec is taking a nap in the GRAND FOYER as he usually does. Perhaps you can take advantage of this and sneak out of the house another way?

> Jade: Grab your harpoon gun.

Oh yes, of course! One of your REMINDERS reminds you that you still have a package to deliver too. This way you can kill two birds with one harpoon gun.

> Jade: Use harpoon to zip-line into the great outdoors.

Killing two birds with one harpoon gun would be one-upping Dave, who earlier killed one bird with one shitty sword.

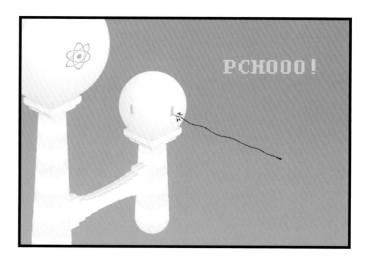

PCHOOO is a sound a gun makes, and that lots of other things make, in *Homestuck*. Learn more about *Homestuck* facts like this, and other *Homestuck* facts, in my Author Notes™.

> Rose: Finish building.

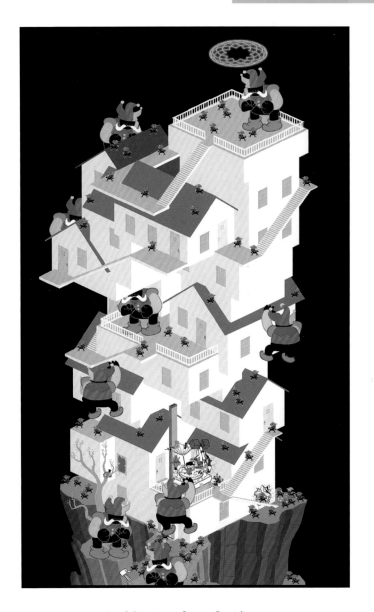

Architectural perfection.

> Dave: Mourn the loss of Cal.

John's house is finally starting to resemble a level in an actual video game, with enemies and everything. It's about time.

See you little dude.

If you had any more APPLE JUICE you would pour some out for your homie.

You'll have to remember to double-check your closet for more juice.

> Dave: Go get a god damn new sword.

Perhaps you will. But if you do, it looks like you'll have to break it first.

Perfectly good STRIFE SPECIBUS, down the toilet. Thanks BRO.

> Dave: Captchalogue beta.

There's no more juice in your closet, Dave. Keep dreaming.

You try to grab the BETA (6) but you forgot your sylladex is completely packed.

You wonder why you jammed all this useless crap in here in the first place. Maybe you assumed you would weaponize it all during one of your customary HASHRAP battles with your BRO. But in retrospect that probably just would have been a huge chore and would have made the battle drag on forever.

It's like what are you made of time.

> Dave: Eject your modus and set it to Scrabble values.

The hashrap battles really would have taken too much time and stretched out the story a bit, so I'm glad I didn't do them. Other things I could have cut out to save time without losing much include: most pages.

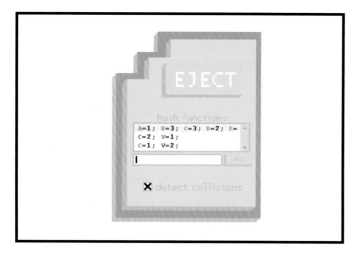

You dump all this crap all over the roof.

You then set your modus to the SCRABBLE HASH FUNCTION for some reason. This function always makes it a little less intuitive to calculate hash values for items, and therefore more cumbersome to rap with. But you guess that's kind of a moot point now that your BRO flew off fuck knows where. His mysterious ways transcend irony once again.

> Dave: Get beta.

You get the BETA (3+1+1+1), now yielding a radically different hash value with the Scrabble function.

Which is to say a radically exactly the same value.

> Dave: Pester Rose.

Generally I have my finger on the pulse of reader desires. Even when I'm not reading their feedback, I can just feel it. It's like a sixth sense. That's how I knew that exactly right about now you were all craving more sylladex shenanigans.

-- turntechGodhead [TG] began pestering
tentacleTherapist [TT] --

TG: ok i got it
TG: i hope you appreciate how much gross
spongy proboscis i had to fellate to get
this game
TG: hello
TG: what are you doing
TG: anyway im going down stairs now and
installing this thing
TG: later

You have finally finished your building project.
You have done about all you can do for John. You
don't think you can provide much assistance against
all those ogres this time, but at least now John
appears to be armed to the teeth.

All there is left to do is wait for Dave.

> Rose: Captchalogue and send John code
for his present.

Gross, spongy proboscis fellatio is a concept that I introduced to you before anyone else did. I guarantee this.

That would certainly hasten the parcel's delivery, but the gift is not finished yet!

You have spent months accelerating your knitting skills to be able to make the gift of perfect sentimental appeal. You even incorporated a cherished heirloom you have had as long as you can remember.

When he sees your staggering gesture of sentimentality he will finally understand. He will understand that in the game of facetious sentimental gestures, no one gets the best of Rose Lalonde.

> Months in the past...

> dear rose,

dear rose,
happy birthday!!!
thanks for being such a great friend all these years. i know you like to make it out like you're playing it cool and don't care much about the people in your life, bu[t] ...... you really do.

(crappy, sorry)

(crappy, sorry)

dear rose,

happy birthday!!!

thanks for being such a great friend all these years. i know you like to make it out like you're playing it cool and don't care much about the people in your life, but i know deep down you really do. hell, not even that deep down. it's like, um, like your subconscious is having a wet t-shirt contest, and you being all aloof is this totally soggy shirt doing no good at all at hiding nothin'. oh wait, it looks like two can play at this game of cracking all these high falutin psychology books! AW SNAP!!!

but yeah, i got you this because i think you're really creative and you could make something nice with it if you put your mind to it. and it might help you take your mind off a lot of all this serious business you're always absorbed in. you know, all this weirdo pseudo-gothy stuff or whatever. frankly it's kind of depressing.

anyway you're the best rose! have a rad 13th! (i will catch up with you guys soon. god you're all so old.)

~ghostyTrickster
(john)

> Rose: Answer.

John, are you.sure that was a high falutin psychology book you cracked, and not a copy of *The Horny Teen's Guide to Confusing Analogies*?

-- **grimAuxiliatrix** [GA] **began trolling tentacleTherapist** [TT] --

GA: Why Is It That When The Subject Of Temporal Mechanics Is Broached Your Sparing Human Intellects Instantly Assume The Most Ingratiating Posture Of Surrender Imaginable
GA: Time Is Not That Difficult To Understand
GA: It Is A Utility That A Universe May Resort To In Order To Advance A Desired Degree Of Complexity
GA: Or May Not Resort To If That Is The Case
GA: Its All Pretty Pedestrian
GA: But No
GA: When Time Travel Comes Up You Present The Face That A Man Shows When The Breeze Gradually Alerts Him To His Absence Of Netherdressings
GA: I Dont See How We Are To Properly Agitate You All If You Continue To Insist On Failing To Understand Basic Concepts Which Common Infants Effortlessly Manage To Describe Via Scrawlings In Their Own Puddles Of Sloppy Discharge
TT: Have we spoken before?
GA: Yes
GA: In The Future
TT: You and your friends never cease to invent ways to strengthen the credibility of your assertions.
GA: Oh My It Is Your Human Sarcasm Again
GA: I Enjoy Listening To It And I Wish Doing So Could Serve As My Primary Form Of Recreation
GA: There See I Just Did It Too
GA: Saying The Opposite Thing To Emphasize My Contempt
GA: But Suddenly I Feel More Primitive And Hate Myself A Little More
GA: It Was Like This Funny Miracle That Just Happened In My Heart
TT: I would admire the sophistication of you and your fellow future-dwellers a little more if you seemed to be aware the word "human" only functions as that sort of adjective in bad science fiction.
TT: But I won't be rude and change the subject.
TT: There's a still a bit of unflagellated straw poking out of your rhetorical effigy over here.
GA: Oh Dear
GA: No We Arent From "The Future"
GA: But We Are All Already In Agreement That You Dont Get It And Never Will
TT: I thought you said we spoke in the future.
GA: We Did
GA: Your Future
GA: For Me It Was Only A Couple Minutes Ago
TT: I understand.

This would be the first extensive conversation with a troll, which, considering how many are to come later, should be looked upon as a significant benchmark. Kanaya—oops, I mean GA—likes to throw around the term "human sarcasm" as if sarcasm is something trolls don't have, when they clearly do. Actually that's pretty much the thrust of all jokes about their cultural differences. Hell, they don't even have different movie stars.

TT: You exist in some temporal stratum through which you have communication access to various points of my timeline.
TT: It's not that complicated.
GA: Yes Thats Right
GA: Will You Try To Talk Some Sense Into Your Idiot Friends
GA: So That We May Proceed To Bother Them All On More Rational Terms
TT: I try to every day, with mixed results.
TT: But you see, it's not that I don't understand you.
TT: It's just that I don't believe you.
TT: Because it's nonsense.
TT: Albeit persistent and coordinated nonsense.
TT: Why would a bunch of temporally dislocated trolls want to harass a group of friends throughout completely random points in time?
GA: I Will Admit This Campaign Of Provocation Wasnt All That Well Thought Out
GA: Dont Tell Anyone I Said That
TT: Alright.
TT: Maybe you should get some trolling tips from us humans.
TT: Our sparing intellects are probably better suited to it.
GA: Yeah Maybe
GA: Why Dont We Be Friends
TT: You want to be my friend?
GA: I Think So
GA: I Think Were Supposed To
GA: You Suggested As Much Earlier
TT: You mean I did in the future?
GA: Yes A Couple Minutes Ago
TT: Probably because I remembered you mentioning it in the conversation we're having now?
GA: Thats Likely
TT: Hmm.
TT: Your commitment to this roleplaying scenario is intriguing.
TT: What choice do I have but to accept?

When she says the campaign of provocation wasn't thought out all that well, she's really just busting on Karkat. That's literally all that's going on here.

> dear dave,

```
dear dave,

happy birthday!!!

i just wanted to take a break from
telling you how much your gay butt
stinks all the time and say what an
awesome friend you are. seriously, on
any other day i would be downplaying
how you aren't really as cool as you
think you are, but just between you
and me i think you might actually be
that cool.
```

i think you just gotta get out of your bro's shadow and spread your wings dude!!!

so i got you these. they're totally authentic! they actually touched ben stiller's weird, sort of gaunt face at some point. i'm sure you'll dig them because i know you lolled so hard at that movie. ok so for real, this is sort of a shitty present, but it is an ironic present because i know you wouldn't have it any other way. maybe you can wear them ironically some time. they MIGHT even be more ironic than you and your bro's dumb pointy anime shades.

anyway, have a good one buddy! and stay busy being totally sweet!

~ghostyTrickster
(john)

> Dave: Answer.

Please note that John here is explicitly urging Dave to become a bird. Stick that fact in your cap for later. Less explicitly he's giving Dave a new look so he can be more distinct from his brother. Personal arcs in the Strider clan tend to have a lot to do with identity. But Snoop Dogg/Lion there would agree, you've got to be you. Uh-oh, here's Tavros.

-- adiosToreador [AT] began trolling turntechGodhead [TG] --

AT: hEYYY,
AT: fIRST, oK, i THINK YOU'RE AWFUL,
AT: lET'S PUT THAT FACT ON THE TABLE WHERE WE CAN BOTH SEE IT,
AT: nOW YOU HAVE BEEN PRIMED FOR THE DIGESTIVE RUINATION THAT'S ABOUT TO TAKE PLACE, aND THE COMPREHENSIVE SOILING OF THE LAUNDRY ENVELOPING YOUR PERSON,
TG: oh my god you type like a tool
AT: yEAHHH,
AT: nOW YOU'RE GETTING IT, wHAT YOU ARE IN FOR,
AT: aRE YOU READY TO BE TROLLLLLED,
AT: wITHIN AN INCH OF YOUR MISERABLE HUMAN CORTEX,
TG: this is so weak im almost getting tired of wasting good material on you guys
TG: its like
TG: youve got nothing
TG: its always one of you sprouting up and ranting about how hard im about to get trolled
TG: with no ensuing substance
TG: you dont even know anything about us
TG: one of you fuckers thought i was a girl
AT: oK, yEAH, bUT,
AT: tHE THING IS, tHAT i DON'T CARE,
AT: aBOUT YOUR ANATOMICAL DETAILS, aND THINGS LIKE THAT,
AT: i KNOW WHAT YOU'VE DONE,
AT: oR WILL DO, aCTUALLY,
AT: iT'S THE MOST AWFUL THING, tHE WORST YOU CAN EVER DO,
TG: sorry i wouldnt cyber with you dude
TG: in the future or whatever
AT: wHAT, wAIT,
AT: oH,
AT: oK, yOU'RE THE ONE WHO LIKES TO SUBMIT INNUENDO,
TG: human innuendo
AT: yES, hUMAN iNNUENDO,
AT: sORRY FOR THE LACK OF CLARITY,
TG: so at what point in the future am i supposed to look forward to you whipping up this titanic hankerin for my knob
AT: uH,
TG: be honest with me
TG: cause im busy
TG: and i want to know exactly when i got to clear some space in my calendar for when some fuckwit blunders out of a magical phone booth and makes a ballad-inspiring play for my throbbing beef truncheon

And here is the first time we see indisputable evidence that troll conversations can be funny. This is a real watershed moment, because it happens a lot later. Well okay, it happens sometimes. Well okay, it happens this time. Also I feel I should point out that when Dave mentions the phone booth, people think I'm referencing *Dr. Who*. But really I (Dave) was thinking more along the lines of *Bill and Ted*. People need to quit all the nerd shit and start boning up on excellent movies.

AT: sHOULD i BE PERTURBED BY THESE ALLUSIONS,
TG: no man
TG: look
TG: i just need to know when to be there
TG: when the stars come into alignment and your flux capacitor lets you finally sate your meteoric greed for crotch-dachshund
TG: i wouldnt want to miss it and cause a paradox or something
TG: itd suck if the universe blew up on account of you missing your window of opportunity to help yourself to a pubescent boy's naked spam porpoise
AT: uHHH,
AT: oK, THIS IS SORT OF STARTING TO UPSET ME,
TG: jesus you are such a shitty troll
AT: i GUESS i'LL LEAVE YOU ALONE,
AT: aND FIND ANOTHER POINT IN TIME TO BOTHER YOU,
AT: wHEN, i GUESS,
AT: yOU ARE MORE EMOTIONALLY SUSCEPTIBLE, aND DON'T HAVE ALL THESE BEES IN YOUR BONNET,
AT: aBOUT YOUR HUMAN SEXUALITY,
TG: oh no
TG: no dude
TG: you sassed me up
TG: we are in THE SHIT now
TG: together
TG: for the long haul
AT: i,
AT: wHAT,
TG: we're motherfuckin entrenched in this bitch
TG: you and me
TG: welcome to nam
TG: now grab my hand and shimmy your soggy ass off that muddy bank before charlie gets the fuckin drop
AT: uHHH, wHO,
AT: wHO'S CHARLIE,
TG: hes the guy whos gonna read our vows
TG: im feeling pretty friggin MATRIMONIAL all a sudden
TG: take a look down by your foot see that little bottle
TG: stomp on that shit like its on fire
TG: noisy ethnic dudes are flipping the fuck out and waving us around on chairs til someone gets hurt
TG: im your 300 pound matronly freight-train
TG: and my gaping furnace is hungry for coal so get goddamn shoveling
AT: oH MY GOD,

As is so often the case with jerky teen males on the internet, Dave's cudgel of choice here appears to be relentless homosexual innuendo. Please note that the phrase "cudgel of choice" may be considered homosexual innuendo as well.

```
TG: bro look in my eyes
TG: that twinkle
TG: that be DEVOTION you herniated pro wrestlers sweaty purple taint
TG: sparklin like a visit from your fairy fuckin godmother
TG: shit be PURE AND TRUE
TG: thats what you see
TG: a kaleidoscopic supernova of all your hopes and dreams all swishin together
TG: radially effevescing arms of more little boy peckers than you can imagine
TG: turning out insane corkscrew haymakers of a billion dancing vienna sausages strong
TG: this is how we do this
TG: this shits more real than kraft mayo

 -- adiosToreador [AT] blocked turntechGodhead [TG] --
```

> You are now...

The Aimless Renegade.

You have identified a couple of unwelcome rogues outside your present stronghold. They are in violation of your jurisdiction. Despite your ordinarily striking marksmanship, you have spent your entire ammo clip without recording a single killshot.

What will you do?

> AR: Realize that your weapon is magazine-fed, not clip-fed.

Dave's joke about mayo STRONGLY foreshadows the friendship he has later with the Mayor.

You don't give a shit about that.

> AR: Examine the wall behind you.

The wall exhibits rows of ancient hieroglyphs depicting an array of amphibious and reptilian life forms.

This is illegal pictography. It makes you angry.

> AR: Go search for more ammo.

Somebody tried to bust me on the clip vs. magazine issue, but I just busted them right back, because wow, who giiiiiiiiiives a shit.

227

There is plenty of ammunition stored in the various **AMMO CRATES** which you have spent a great deal of time unearthing from nearby dunes and hauling back to your stronghold. You have a large variety of weaponry and ammunition at your disposal.

Whether you can locate some more AK47 rounds quickly enough is a different matter.

> AR: Quickly retrieve side arms.

You retrieve a pair of deadly **SIDE ARMS**.

But you will need a longer-ranged weapon if you are to continue your enforcement.

> AR: Find a rocket launcher.

Here's one.

> AR: Befriend the unwelcome rogues.

AR: Retrieve deudly firearms. Wait, that joke hasn't been made yet. AR: Wait for that joke to be made.

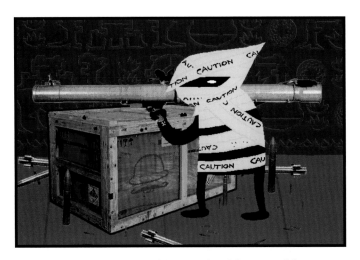

You wonder if you should reconsider your grievance with the offenders. Perhaps you should let it slide? They seem friendly enough, and it's been so long since you've had company. It would also be quite a pity to blow up that tall attractive female.

But then again...

They are both in flagrant violation, trespassing through several zones which you painstakingly marked as off-limits while you conduct your investigation of this crime scene. It is your duty to investigate this ILLEGAL MONUMENT and get to the bottom of its ILLICIT AMPHIBIOUS IDOLATRY. Just thinking about all the sloppy footprints they are leaving in the sand makes your carapace steam.

The law is all that's left to hold on to in this unforgiving dust bowl. You cannot afford to loosen your black claw's grip lest justice slip through your fingers. Law is beauty. Order is peace. Judgment is the very basis for all that is pure and...

Hold that thought.

You need to take a moment to wear something ridiculous before you continue your spiel...

I ship AR x Terezi because of their mutual interest in justice, and AR x PM because of his explicitly stated attraction to her. I am a simple shipper who is easy to please, folks.

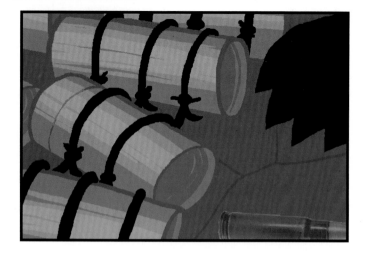

ORDER IN THE COURT. YOU WILL HAVE ORDER IN THIS COURTROOM. IF EVERYONE DOES NOT SETTLE DOWN YOU WILL CLEAR OUT THIS COURTROOM, YOU SWEAR TO GOD.

> AR: Examine moving platform.

It appears to be a large stage serving as a kind of elevator. But it can't go down because there's something jammed in it. Looks like a peculiar musical instrument, probably centuries old.

But yeah, the jury agrees. You've got to go blow up those trespassers.

> Jade: Place present on monument.

Jade's ancient, rusted bass getting lodged in the elevator gives the musical euphemism "jamming" a new meaning. Wait, was that joke not funny? Oops. Sorry.

You put John's present down in just the right spot, along with a letter you prepared a little while ago after a particularly interesting series of dreams.

Should be any minute now...

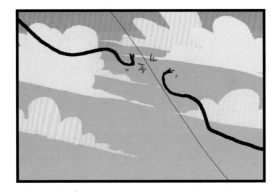

You put down the time-bait. It's out of your hands now.

Jade isn't even looking through the scope there. She's no-scoping that skinny cable from like a hundred yards. Damn, she's good.

(Mary. Fucking. SUE.)

You guess you could swim.

Maybe you can think of a better way across though.

This is kind of confusing.

> PM: Read the letter.

But you guess it's straightforward enough, even if the drawing is somewhat inaccurate...

PM: There's no hole in the left side of that helicopter thing, and that stone column is still standing. Realize the diagram is useless and discard it.

Oh no!

> AR: Berate self for unauthorized demolition.

STUPID STUPID STUPID

You had them right in your crosshairs.
You have no idea how a crack shot
like you could have missed. It is
practically inconceivable.

> AR: Be the law.

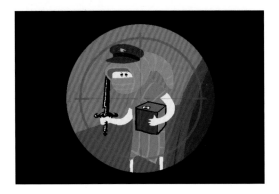

You reload and take aim.

That fair carapace... how it sparkles
in the desert light.

No. You cannot afford to be distracted
by such thoughts. You are busy being
the law.

Law: Get been by AR.

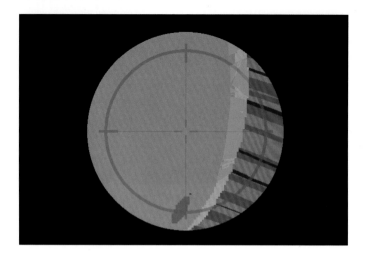

YOU ARE THE LAW WHOOPS

> WV: Wave about in a distracting manner.

Oh it's this guy again and his little blinking bee.
So outrageous.

Subtle Trivia: did you know the "LoB" sound effect is written with lettering kinda similar to the Tab logo?

THE CAN RUSE WAS A...........

DISTACTION

> PM: Scamper quickly to the newly created hole.

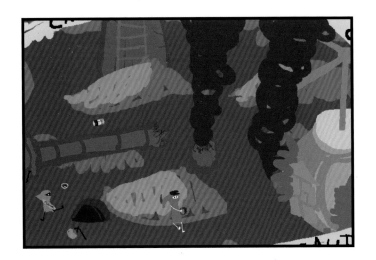

you HAVE
the cargo

Did you know that if you press hard enough on the *SBaHJ* text up there with your finger, the book will open up the comic it's referencing in a new browser window?

235

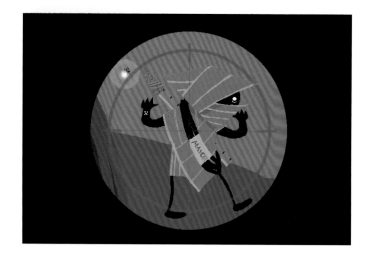

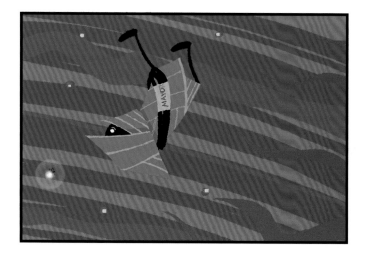

> PM: Read the next step of the letter.

I think AR may be getting an unfair share of the blame for his poor markmanship. The rocket launcher might be showing its age here. The paths some of these rockets are taking are BULLSHIT.

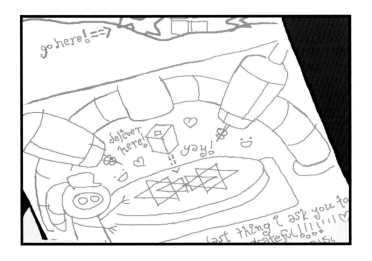

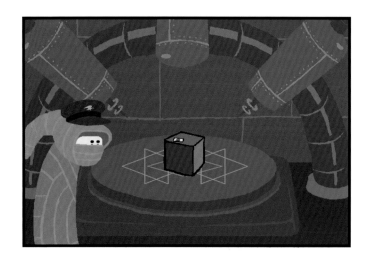

At the bottom of the letter is a series of coordinates along with further instructions.

You know what you must do.

Liberty. Reason. Justice. Civility. Edification. Perfection.

> Years in the past...

Today is your BIRTHDAY. Your grandfather has decided to celebrate by introducing you to THE THRILL OF THE HUNT.

But suddenly you and Bec are wandering off. Where is this silly DOG taking you?

You find a PRESENT.

You open it to find a shirt that is way too big for you, and... pumpkin seeds?

There is also a letter.

> dear jade,

dear jade,

happy birthday!!!

it's hard to thank you enough for your friendship over the years. heck, if it weren't for you i wouldn't even have met rose and dave, so that is like, THREE TIMES the friendship! that is almost like, TOO MUCH FRIENDSHIP. ha ha. i only wish i could get you something for your birthday that could remotely make up for what you've given me, but of course that's impossible. so here are a couple silly things anyway!

i went to a weird asian store the other day and saw this rad shirt, so i got it and i'm wearing it now! but there was a blue one too which was way more awesome, and i wanted you to have it. i know you like green a lot, but maybe you'd like to try wearing blue sometimes? i bet you'd look like a million bucks! also i know you've been frustrated lately about how your pumpkins keep disappearing. well, i can't begin to explain why that's happening! all i can do is give you these so you can plant some more. don't give up, jade! wherever those dumb old pumpkins went off to, i'm sure you know the fun is in growing them and taking care of them until they're ready!

whew, got to head out to the post office now so this doesn't get to you TOO late! talk to you soon!!!

~ghostyTrickster
(john)

Who is this John claiming to be your friend?
And these other friends he mentions?

Whoever he is, you think he might be on to
something. Blue is a very pretty color! Also,
growing some pumpkins sounds like it could be
fun. Maybe you will ask Grandpa if you can
use the atrium to do some gardening. This
will be exciting.

> WHOP

You bear the vicious brunt of this story transition directly in the face.

You are getting really tired of this feisty man and his busy fists.

> Jack: Kill John's dad yourself.

Jade is pretty good at reading for a two-year-old. Let's just assume she's two and move on.

Here, stick this in your pipe and bleed to death slowly.

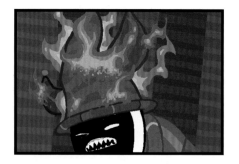

This is the biggest fuck-you imaginable coming from Dad. There is no greater sign of disrespect than setting a man's hat on fire, slathering it in Barbasol, and stomping on it.

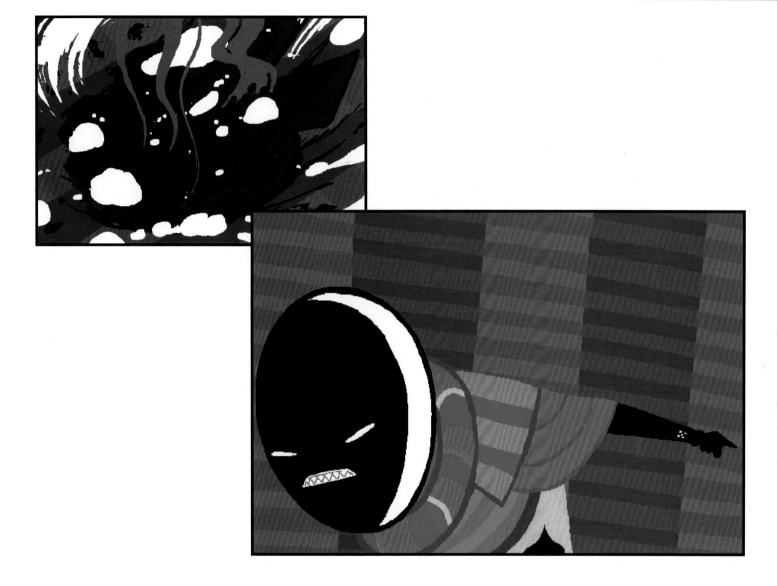

You release the prisoner. He is free to go.

> Jade: Play guitar to summon giant lily pads.

Little did he realize it would only earn Jack's admiration and gratitude. (For now.)

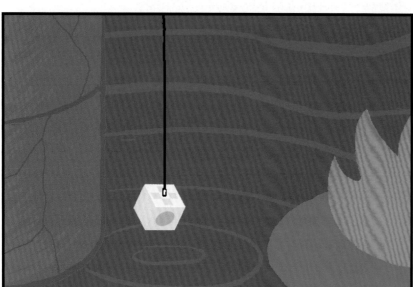

Jade's earlier use of the bass + amplifier to grow the vegetables foreshadowed this extremely significant moment, where she uses the same technique to grow a lily pad bridge. The goofy cartoon frog Jade I guess foreshadows frogs, which come up again later in the story, but I forget why. It's not that important.

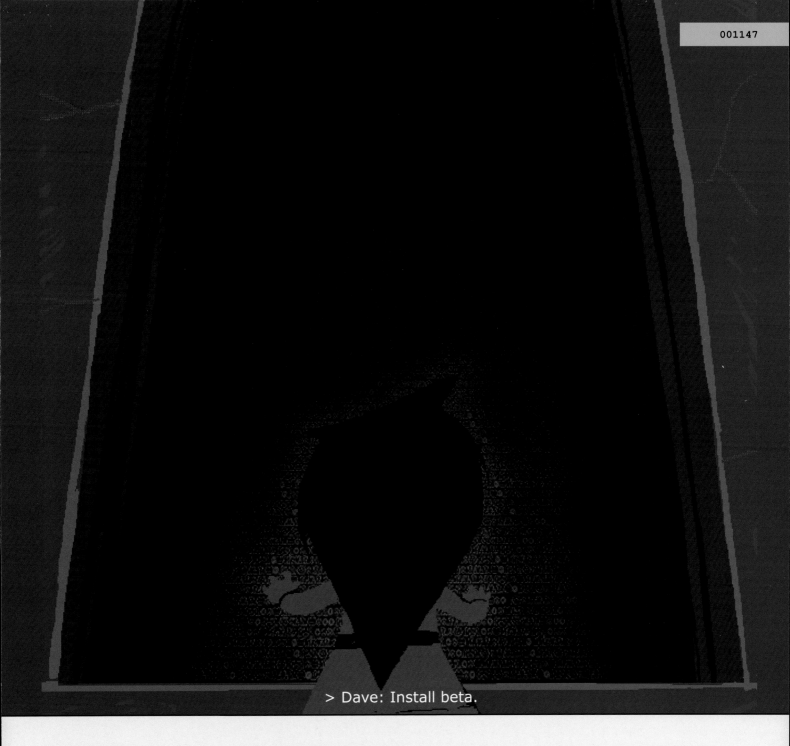

> Dave: Install beta.

Does the long pattern of runes on the temple wall represent the code for *Sburb*? Or maybe the entire genome for Bilious Slick?? Neither. It is a magic eye diagram, and when you unfocus your eyes, you can read the word "ribbit."

245

TG: alright im installing this game finally
TT: Where doing this man?
TG: yeah
TG: you could almost say
TG: where making this
TT: Go on.
TT: What is it where making this?
TG: TRANSPIRE
TG: 😎
TT: Excellent.
TT: Let's make shit take place.

>[S] Enter.

They are lampshading *Sweet Bro and Hella Jeff*, which itself is already lampshading good taste and quality aesthetic judgment. In *Homestuck* there are so many lampshades, there is no room left for actual lamps.

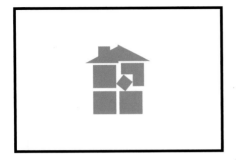

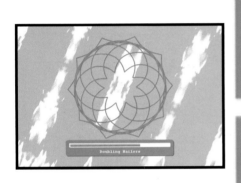
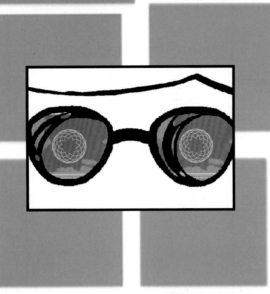

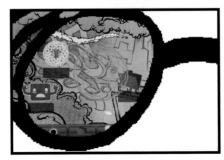

Here is the beginning of the End of Act animation **[S] Enter**. Panels are sliding around the screen. They're showing stuff. Things are happening. It's exciting.

Look at how I was still switching her shirt logo around even in the middle of an animation sequence. This is called attention to detail.

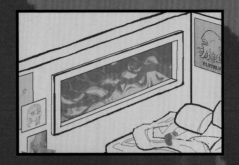

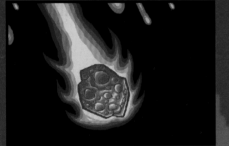
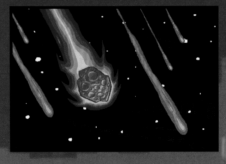

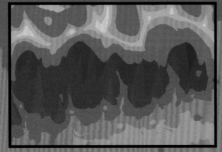
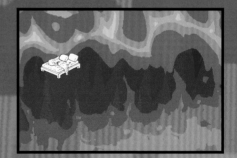

And there goes the bed. If only the bed could have burned to death on its Quest Bedbed.

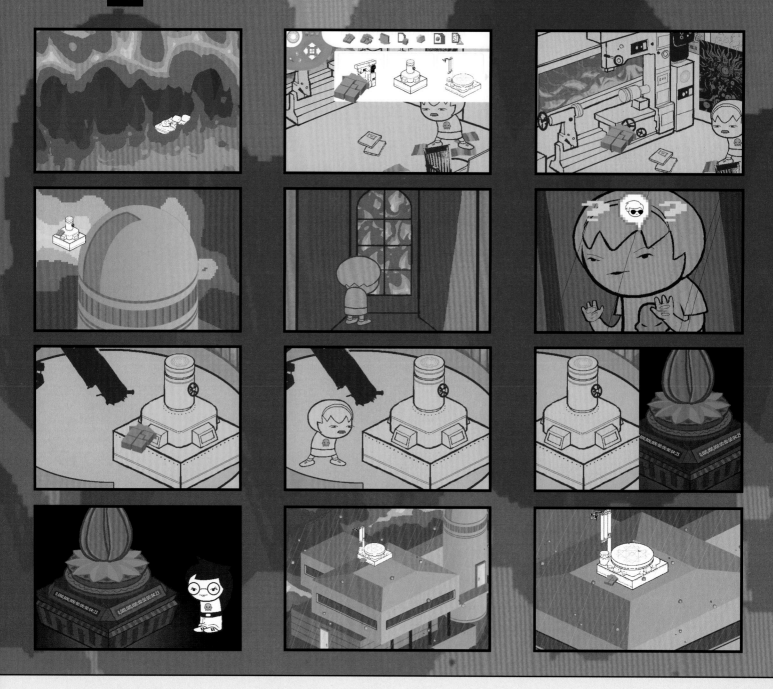

All this stuff goes by pretty quickly in the animation, so maybe we can appreciate it being slowed down here and really let it soak in. Look at Dave putting all this stuff in these terrible inconvenient locations. What a jackass!

The real hero of Act 3: a twenty-foot tall, ten-ton stone statue of Zazzerpan the Learned. Those Zazzerstats are canon, BTW.

Rose was eager to play this game in the first place so she could resurrect her dead cat, AND GODDAMN IT THAT'S EXACTLY WHAT SHE'S GOING TO DO. All these flaming tornadoes and flying wizards can go to hell.

There's this whole spiel on *Sburb*'s "entry items" and what they mean, which I won't get into now. But here's another brief spin on it. John's item is an apple from a tree, obviously like the one from the Bible. In that tale, the apple symbolizes temptation to Adam and Eve, and trouble is a-lurkin' if they take a bite. The liquor bottle similarly represents a kind of temptation in the context of Rose's character arc.

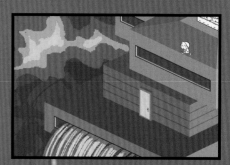

At the end of almost every act in *Homestuck*, something happens that brings the act back full circle. Act 3 started with Nanna's inscription to John, and here we see when and how that was written, while also getting a very brief glimpse of what's under the clouds, and thus a peek at the much bigger story waiting to be discovered.

One wonders if Rose was aware Dave had given Jaspers some useful tentacles to bail her out with before she jumped. It was quite a leap of faith. Or just outright suicidal. The Lalondes and Striders are basically all cuckoo bananas. But anyway, let's reflect on the teamwork involved to make everything work. Rose bringing Jaspers back, Dave making him a princess, Jaspers saving Rose... God, teamwork is great. So is friendship. If your story isn't in some way basically about friendship and teamwork, you are failing hilariously at your job.

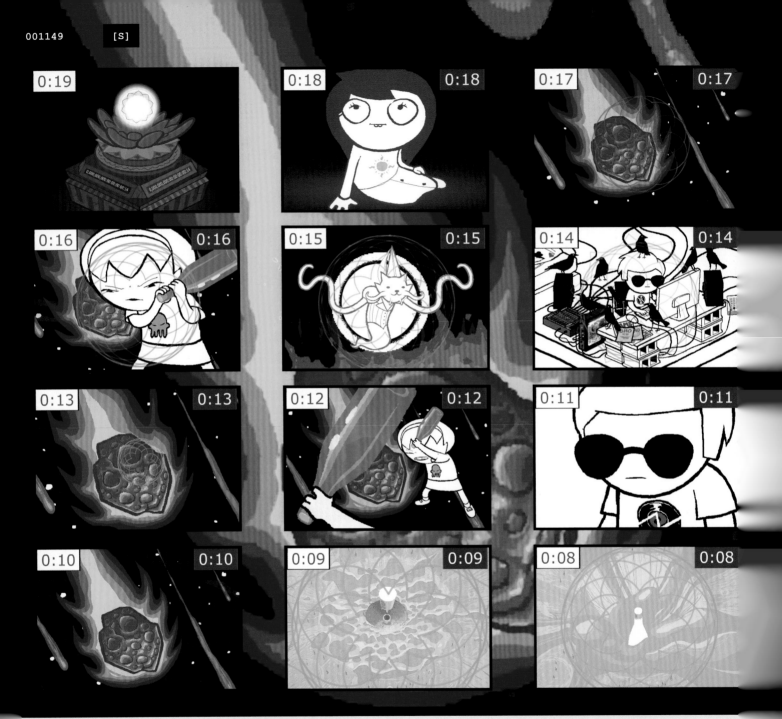

At the bottom of this montage we see a very quick rewind of WV blasting off in his big can. Which turns out to be the cork of a huge bottle, the unsurprising shape of the exile station that formed in Rose's crater. Exile station designs are based on the entry item of the player at that location. As if you didn't know that already.

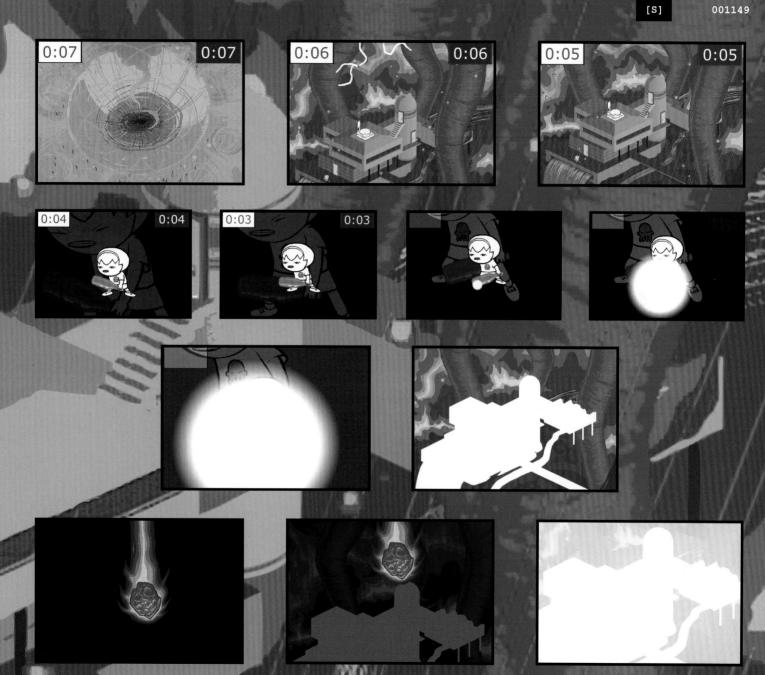

Sure cuttin' it close there, Rose...

My characters never listen to me.

During this frenetic animation, crazy story revelations are strobe-lighting into your brain every few seconds, and you can barely keep up. Here they are delivered at the speed of BOOKS, which is to say, the speed of a sloth swimming through a tar pit. The thing being revealed here: Dave's copy of the game has been stored in this lotus time capsule for millions of years. WHAT?? Yes, the same juice-stained copies currently on the roof below his window. How do they get here? This is how most mysteries work in *Homestuck*. You know a thing is going to happen in the future, but you don't know why or how. So you just keep reading, while screaming.

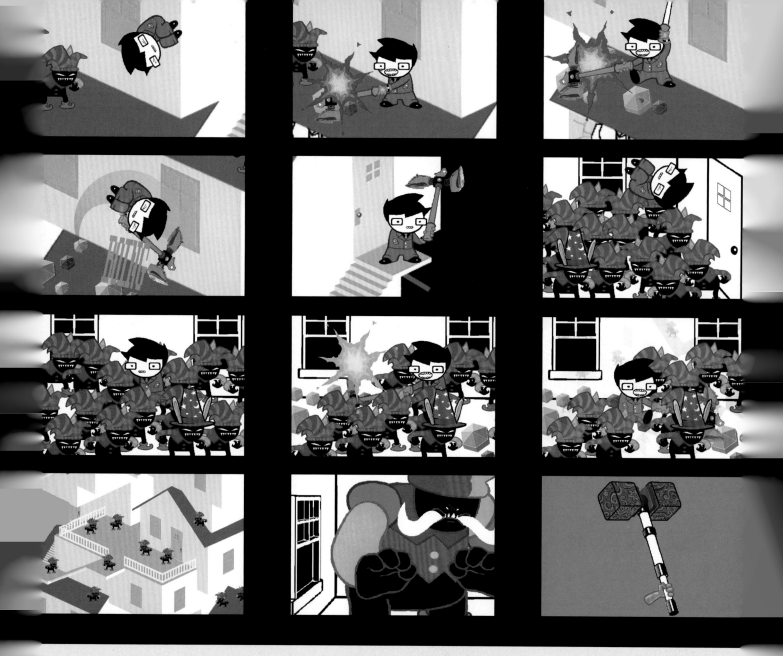

e animation just keeps on going, and the song "Sburban Jungle" sorta bumps it up a notch. John proceeds to climb his house while kicking imp and ogre ass. There
e a few moments in the earlier acts that seem to trick you into thinking *Homestuck* is all about getting cool gear, gaining levels, and kicking ass like you expect to do
such games. This is kind of misleading, though. In totality, HS isn't really about ass-kicking at all. It's about presenting awesome fantasy environments and situations
which ass-kicking could THEORETICALLY take place but very rarely does except in dramatic hot points like this. Instead, those environments serve as backdrops for a
ge amount of dicking around on the internet, babbling to friends about feelings, and being a bunch of stupid, useless kids struggling to grow up. If you are ever under
e impression HS is about anything else, you are invariably in for a world of hurt.

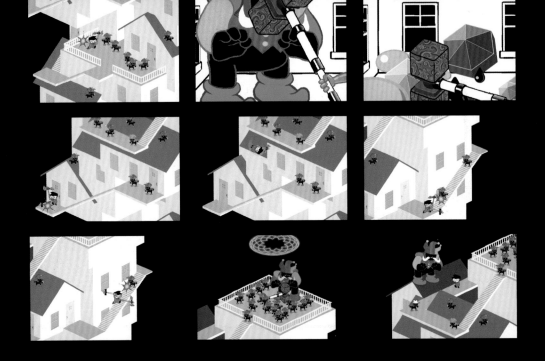

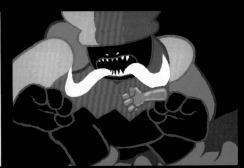

The best part of the animation is when John just runs up and clocks a hapless imp in the face. Don't even try to tell me it isn't.

Whereas this imp gets inadvertently Cosby'd into the pit. You'd think John would later find the Cosbytop lying around somewhere down there, but I don't think that's what happens. I think he just makes another one?? Why the hell not. The great thing about alchemy is that it puts very little premium on almost any single object. Except ones which are plot critical enough to be unique, like the game disc, or the matriorb. It's almost like...the game knows when an item is plot critical?? It's almost like...my brain as the author of the story IS the game???

Then John boings into the thing. The end.

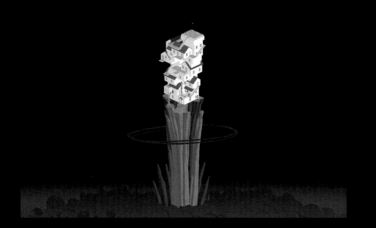

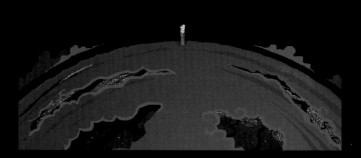

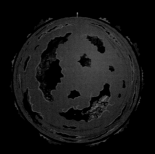

> END OF ACT 3

We zoom way out from John's house, and for the first time we understand that this mysterious realm is actually a whole planet. After this point we get kinda used to the ever-expanding cosmological scale of the story, but let's slap our jaded faces for a second here, take a step back, and realize this is all pretty cool. Wow, all the kids who play the game get their own special planet? Wow, neat! Actually, we can't conclude that formally until we see Rose's planet appear later. Until then, people are likely to (and did) speculate that her house will appear somewhere on this cloudy planet. But no. Let's slap our faces again for jumping to that conclusion.

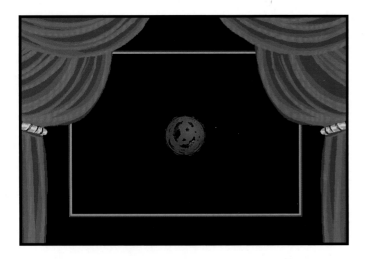
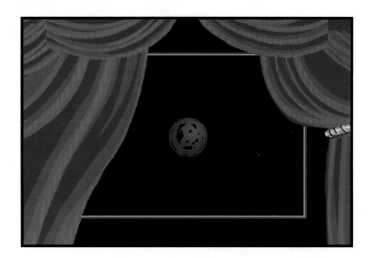

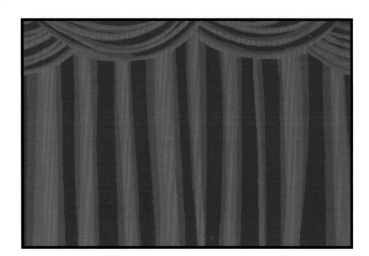

> INTERMISSION

Bye, Act 3. The Midnight Crew Intermission is next! If anecdotal evidence can be trusted, you will either read that section ten times, or you will skip it altogether. Skipping it would be a huge mistake, though, trust me. Almost as big a mistake as it was to get involved with *Homestuck* in the first place.

INTERMISSION
DON'T BLEED ON THE SUITS

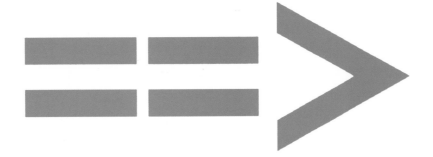

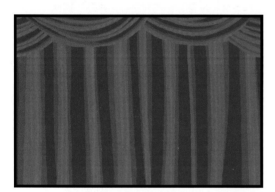

All right, who's ready for the Midnight Crew Intermission??? I know I was when I made it. By this point, it was very clear to me how different it felt to make *Homestuck* than it did making the prior story, *Problem Sleuth*. *Homestuck* was much more labor-intensive, and more maniacally constructed and planned in terms of system design, world building, and density of detail. Not to mention the rapidly escalating animation demands. After finishing Act 3 I wanted to mix in some action that felt more like *Problem Sleuth*—lighter on animation, heavier on silly bullshit, and more driven by reader commands. The result is a thing that's indisputably super-duper good and funny. But at the time, it did read as a radical departure from *Homestuck*'s story arc. This is misleading, though. Virtually every idea and character introduced here turns out to be important later on. The Felt's mysterious and elusive mob boss in particular.

Your name is SPADES SLICK. You are the leader of a notoriously vicious gang of mobsters
called the MIDNIGHT CREW. A rival gang known as THE FELT recently knocked over one of
your favorite casinos. Your long quest of revenge has finally taken you through the
front door of the mansion belonging to their loathsome boss, LORD ENGLISH.

Your subordinates, CLUBS DEUCE, DIAMONDS DROOG, and HEARTS BOXCARS have been dispatched
to various locations throughout the mansion to begin carrying out your mission. Your
objective is to locate and crack English's SECRET VAULT, and plunder its mysteries.

That's the business end of it. The pleasure will be painting this ugly house
red with the blood of those miserable green motherfuckers.

> SS: Inspect timekeeping devices.

Maybe I mentioned earlier that Spades Slick was once a noncanon *Problem Sleuth* villain in some bonus content requested by a reader? I don't remember if I
mentioned that. I don't remember what I had for fucking breakfast today. Please bear with me. I decided to appropriate the character as a *Homestuck* villain by
stripping his gangster duds, naming him Jack Noir, and immersing him in some lore about carapacians and fancy kingdoms. But now, confusingly, here's Jack again,
in his old Midnight Crew attire, under his former alias, about to go on a silly mansion caper. What is GOING ON? This is confusing. Or isn't it? (Yes.) Confusing, but
more importantly, COMPREHENSIBLE given enough of your time and attention to this horseshit, god willing.

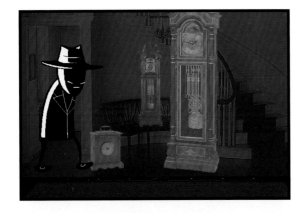

Stupid gang and their lousy obsession with clocks. The sooner all these idiots stop being alive the better.

You wonder where they are. It's awfully quiet in the mansion, sans all the dreadful ticking.

> SS: Captchalogue carriage clock.

You obviously have no idea what that means.

If it's some smartass way of saying to pick it up, forget it. You are already carrying an item. It is your trusty DECK OF CARDS.

> SS: Build fort with clocks.

You have an idea that is so much better.

CLOCKS DESTROYED: 4/1000

> SS: Check for traps under the billiards rug.

Slick, like Jack, is a very surly customer. He's just as ticked (heh heh clock pun) at Lord English for knocking over his casino as Jack is when he's forced to wear a stupid hat. Slick develops grudges easily and clings to them eternally. In fact, though this intermission subplot is fleeting, his quest to avenge his casino literally lasts up until the final moments of *Homestuck*.

What is under the rug is much worse than any trap you can imagine.

It is a member of a species that you do not recognize, with a ghastly furred upper lip.

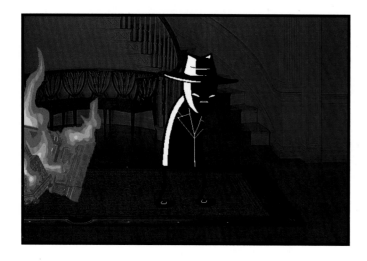

You cover the unsightly individual back up and try to forget it ever existed.

> SS: Play 52 pickup.

You would need a DECK OF CARDS to play that infernal game.

Fortunately all you have is your WAR CHEST, which you deploy on the floor.

> SS: Open war chest.

The mysterious FLOOR FOXWORTHY is there because, of course, its presence is unarguably hilarious. But it serves another important purpose. It lets us know that Slick, unlike Jack, is unfamiliar with humans. He's never seen one before. In case we were wondering what the deal is with this guy, and what his relationship is to Jack Noir, this scene helps us begin to understand that though he's based on the same character template, he is a totally different character.

> SS: Shuffle contents of war chest.

You rummage around. It's no unusual
assortment of belongings, and nothing any
mobster worth his salt would be caught
plotting and scheming without. Certainly
nothing eyebrow raising.

Bunch of blades, some playing cards,and
a variety of other miscellaneous stuff.

Also your VENDETTA ITINERARY and your
HEIST MAP.

> SS: Scavenge war chest for
fancy headwear.

The Crosbytop is another peculiar presence here. But in time we see it has a perfectly traceable origin. (Dad's wallet --> Cal --> Aradia...) I guess we never quite find
out how it specifically came into Slick's possession. It is left to the reader to compose an extremely moving fan fiction to bridge this yawning gorge in canon.

If there are any elaborate headdresses in here, you'll eat your haberdasher.

But of course there is only a plain and serviceable BACKUP HAT, which naturally conceals two LICORICE SCOTTY DOGS.

Which makes you think that maybe you are wearing your BACKUP HAT, and this is your usual one? Hell if you know. They are the same damn hat.

> SS: Hide inside your war chest.

You cannot hide properly inside the chest because you cannot close it while you are inside.

Instead you momentarily pretend it is a really cool automobile that commands the fear and respect of larcenous adversaries everywhere.

BEEP BEEP BEEP

All aboard the idiot wagon!

> SS: Start up the Crosbytop.

The two pieces of candy stored in his hat are a nod to Problem Sleuth, who kept two pieces of candy corn in his hat for the entire story and finished off the final form of last boss with them. Each member of the Midnight Crew has their own kind of candy stashed in their hat.

Is that what this thing is? You've had it for some time, and don't quite remember how you got it. You never knew the identity of this pipe-smoking creature.

Perhaps it could be the same species as the character you just saw under the rug. But you know that is impossible, because this one does not feature the same bizarre furred lip. They are probably differing species within the same genus.

> SS: Go to mspaintadventures.com.

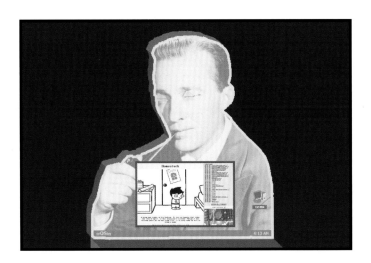

You don't know why you are wasting time on this website. It is for little children who poop hard in their baby ass diapers.

Also you don't understand what the hell is going on or who all these characters are. It's all a lot of nonsense.

> SS: Delete the time setting on the Crosbytop.

Notice that while in our universe MSPA.com is running *Homestuck*, with a Midnight Crew intermission and all, in this universe MSPA runs a Midnight Crew adventure, with a weird mock-*Homestuck* story as an intermission. (Later to be adapted as Homosuck... Let's uh, not get into Homosuck just yet though.)

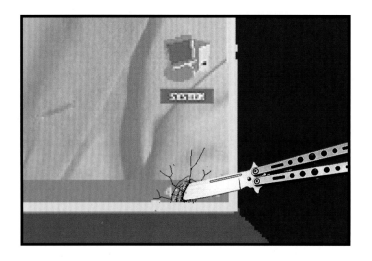

CLOCKS DESTROYED: 5/1000

> SS: Take the spade key.

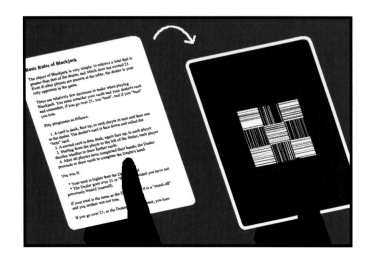

You take the RULES CARD FOR BLACKJACK.

You have possessed this item for as long as you
can remember. You do not yet know its significance.
Though you can hustle up a mean game of blackjack
when you need to.

> SS: Examine vendetta itinerary.

Again like in *Problem Sleuth*, most of these items enjoy object duality. They are either an item/weapon—like a knife, key, or such—or they are one of fifty-two playing cards, which can be stored easily in a deck. Whether they appear as an item or a card depends a lot on the context, which revolves entirely around which form would be most inconvenient, confusing, or aggravating for it to occupy at any given moment.

These are the mugshots of everyone you are going to kill.

You got a head start. You already offed CROWBAR (7), MATCHSTICKS (11), and QUARTERS (14),
depleting them of some of their muscle. You've still got to watch out for the others,
and stay wary of their despicable time shenanigans.

ITCHY (1) has given you the slip repeatedly. DOZE (2) you've captured and interrogated just as
repeatedly, to no avail. TRACE (3) has broken into your secret hideout more times than you can count,
while FIN (5) always seems to be a step ahead of you and scoops your heists. CLOVER (4) has all the
intel and is highly cooperative. You might need him to crack the vault. He'll be guarded. Best to avoid
DIE (6) in any direct confrontations unless you want a temporal mess on your hands. But if you need any
repairs, you could always get to STITCH (9) and "persuade" him. And you might need to if you can't kill
SAWBUCK (10) with a clean shot. EGGS (12) and BISCUITS (13) are morons. But they are dangerous morons.
CANS (15) is a tank and your crew'll probably need more ammunition than you packed to take him down.

No one knows what LORD ENGLISH looks like. But that'll be corrected tonight.

You've got dibs on English. He's all yours.

> SS: Wonder where the number 8 mugshot went.

Here we are introduced to mug shots of the cult fan-favorite gang of time-traveling mobsters known as the Felt. The arc of this intermission as a whole has an uncharacteristically clear objective by *Homestuck* standards. Slick is supposed to kill all of these guys one by one, then finally encounter Lord English and kill him. (LMAO at this notion. It's a nice thought though, Slick.) The fun of this caper involves getting to know these morons, seeing their stupid powers in play, and generally getting swept up in the delirious idiocy of the resulting time shenanigans until everything goes to shit. So, somewhat a microcosm of *Homestuck* itself. In fact, this intermission turns out to be a great primer that helps brace the reader for keeping up with a lot of insane time-travel nonsense that quickly picks up steam soon after.

It's right here.

But you aren't gonna kill SNOWMAN (8).

It's out of the question.

> SS: Examine heist map.

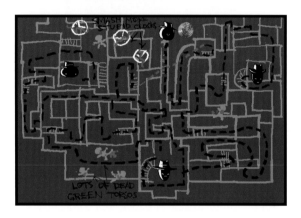

On review, your schemes seem a bit convoluted. But you wouldn't have it any other way.

Deuce and Droog split up to neutralize as many Felt as they can find. Your heavy muscle and expert safecracker, Boxcars, is headed straight down to the vault.

> SS: Use radio device to check on unscrupulous cohorts.

You put the word out to your cronies for a status report. No response yet.

You clean up all your junk and prepare to get this show on the road.

Snowman is hella ominous and mysterious and, unlike her name would suggest, is not a guy. I won't say who she really is, even though you probably already know. For once I'll try to show some discipline and talk about the big reveals in this book when they actually happen. Instead, and much more interestingly, I'll talk about her name, and the names of all the Felt members. Snowman is a card-playing term for an 8 (since it looks like a snowman). All Felt names refer to their numbers. Itchy (Japanese for 1), Doze and Trace (Spanish for 2 and 3), Clover (4-leaf clover), Fin (slang for a 5-dollar bill), Die (standard dice have 6 sides), Crowbar (shaped like a 7), Stitch (in time saves 9), Sawbuck (slang for a 10-dollar bill), Matchsticks (11 looks like couple of matches)...

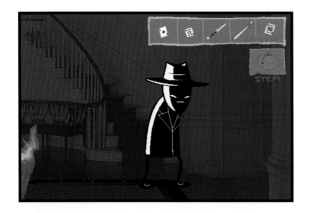

You slip the SPADE KEY back into the DECK
OF CARDS, then pocket the WAR CHEST.

Smooth as clockwork, and every bit as logical.

> SS: Enter the hallway near the
main entrance.

Funny, you didn't hear any commotion or gunplay.
But it looks like there's already been some
action in here. Or there will be. You can never
take tense for granted with these goons.

13/1000 CLOCKS DESTROYED. Apparently.

Looks like Clubs Deuce is getting back to you.

He says he's got Doze tied up for interrogation.

You ask him what else is new. Capturing that guy
is like shooting a paralyzed monkey in the face.

> SS: Be Hearts Boxcars.

...Eggs (typically sold in a carton of 12), Biscuits (13 is a baker's dozen), Quarters and Cans (French for 14 and 15). Also, all their names generally have something to do with their powers. Itchy is fast, Doze is slow, Trace follows, Clover is lucky, Crowbar...has a crowbar. You decide this is all unspeakably clever. Now these dumb green guys are all your favorite characters forever. Oh look, while I was explaining all their names, some funny stuff happened over the last two pages that I don't have room to comment on anymore. Why does this story have to be packed with so much incredible shit worthy of author commentary? It's infuriating, TBH.

You are now Clubs Deuce.

> CD: Rough him up.

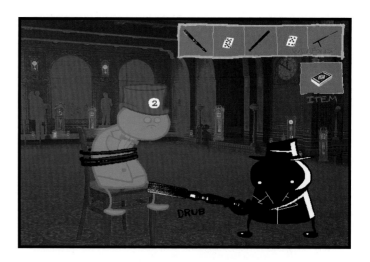

He remains tight-lipped, so you deal him a senseless shin-drubbing with your CROOK OF FELONY.

Oh the humanity. You can barely watch.

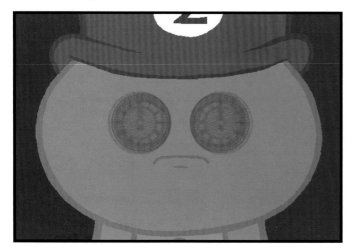

He's probably still using his special ability to slow time down for himself.

He can't feel a damn thing, and certainly isn't saying anything. Apart from a very low noise which could be him saying "ow" very, very slowly.

> CD: Punch clocks in faces to establish chronology.

The first guy we meet isn't #1, but #2, possibly because he is the most objectively useless member of the Felt. He's more useless than the ones who don't even have powers, since his powers are a liability to himself and others. Actually, that's true of all their powers, but only because they're all pretty stupid and don't know what they're doing at all.

Why would you do that? All of these
clocks are lovely. You see no reason
to harm them.

987/1000 CLOCKS UNHARMED

> CD: Swap hats with Doze.

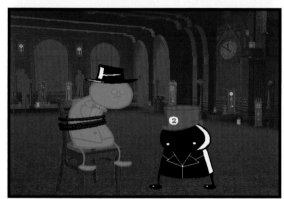

You begin a feeble campaign of psychological
warfare. Perhaps compromising his fashion
motif is the way to get to him.

Nope. Looks like he's still in his weird
state of stasis and doesn't care.

Either that or it's driving him nuts.
Just very slowly.

> CD: Dump the contents of your
war chest over him.

War chest? What are you talking about. All you've got is this simple, unassuming DECK OF CARDS.

> CD: Play some solitaire.

The MC members all have a large receptacle for their gear, which is an object double for a deck of cards. The cards (items) fit into the deck (receptacle) the way a bunch of items (cards) would fit into a large receptacle (deck). Understand now? That's fine, neither does Clubs Deuce. Anyway, their storage receptacles are all these funny plays on words involving bellicose terms like war chest, battledrobe, etc.

Don't be stupid. To play solitaire
you'd need a DECK OF CARDS.

I don't see a DECK OF CARDS, do you?
All I see is your BATTLEDROBE.

> CD: Throw the hat down and
stomp it mercilessly.

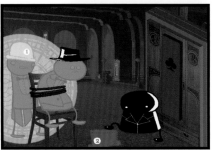  

Oh no. It's Itchy, and it looks like he's all wound up.

He unties Doze and quickly swaps everyone's HATS around.

Doze proceeds to make a fleetfooted getaway.

THE CHASE

IS ON

> SS: Stop being Hearts Boxcars.

Battledrobe is such a perfectly dumbass term since wardrobe already includes the word "war" in it. But I guess Slick already had the war chest and it wouldn't look good to bite the boss's style. Clubs Deuce probably racked his brain coming up with a cool alternative... Fracasdrobe? Scrumdrobe? Altercationdrobe? Also, note how these are just cloned and darkened items from earlier in the story. Slick's chest is John's magic chest. Clubs's battledrobe is Jade's wardrobifier. The other two are repurposed objects as well.

Alright, you're the boss. Hearts Boxcars you ain't.

Someone has replaced your plain and serviceable HAT with a silly and undersized one. An outrage beyond compare.

You're sure you know who the culprit was. You can still smell his overly caffeinated blood...

986/1000 CLOCKS SHOWN MERCY

> SS: Lift left leg and hold it a little ways in the air.

Oops.

Itchy just fucked with the wrong man's hat. He's about to pay the ultimate price (horse hitcher drubbings). And again we see that Jack is a simple man, no matter what name he goes by. He is, if not much else (and he's not), impatient and violent. We only got the briefest glimpse into these qualities when we were first introduced to him on Derse. But now we get to spend more time with him, albeit in the form of a completely different character. This is another bit of sneaky utility provided by this intermission tangent. It serves as an arc to help indirectly characterize the villain of the early acts. Having multiple copies of a character operating in totally different circumstances turns out to be a great stealth characterization tactic, and it gets used much more aggressively later in the story. In fact, it proves to be inseparable from one of the story's most essential themes.

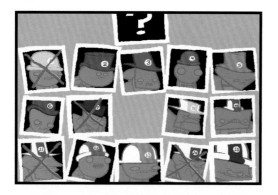

4/15 GREEN TORSOS DEAD

> SS: Wear CD's hat on top of your current one.

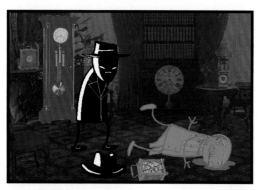

You are already wearing Deuce's hat you fool. The one on the floor is Droog's hat. This is exactly why you always keep a BACKUP HAT on hand.

This son of a bitch on the floor here has played his last game of musical hats. Soon these lugs will learn to show you some respect. You made this town what it is after all. Wasn't nothin' but a bunch of dust and rocks before you got here.

> SS: Wear backup hat.

You deploy your chest and swap this dinky little hat for one more suited to your tastes.

Wait a minute...

Thank god. Your precious SCOTTY DOGS are still here.
You don't know what you'd do without them. You don't want to even think about it.

Itchy, we hardly knew ye. Shame to see him go so soon, but you know what? It's great he died instantly. Now we know Jack/Slick doesn't fuck around and straight-up does not give a fuck about anything. (Except for those moments when he does fuck around and cares a great deal about stupid things like small licorice dogs.) Also, pay attention to the phrase "you made this town." He's not kidding. It's a small clue to a mystery that you don't know is a mystery yet. That's one of the good things about this intermission. Its entire conceit is grounded in the overt representation of clear and present uselessness to *Homestuck*'s story arc. The mystery you are sifting through gradually as you read it, and how it fits into the bigger picture, is why it's not useless. At the very end, when you see the panel of Karkat, is when you find out.

Die makes his usual sort of entrance. The nonplussed, vaguely bewildered sort.

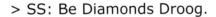

> SS: Be Diamonds Droog.

You got it. Clubs Deuce it is.

You have opened your BATTLEDROBE in search of your BACKUP HAT. You also need some more ROPE to retie Doze, who is absolutely tearing through the mansion as we speak. If you don't hurry, he may clear the chair within the hour.

But it's a big mess. You mostly just see a bunch of bombs and cards.

Die appears because he just stuck a yellow Itchy pin in the doll, thus jumping to a timeline in which he's dead. But we'll find that out in a few pages. For now, let me direct your attention to the bull penis cane that just fell out of the battledrobe. Why am I directing your attention to it? I just am. It becomes incredibly important later by appearing in a funny panel, as a joke. No need to thank me, just doing my job.

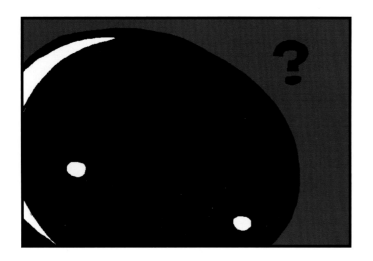

You're not sure what's what. You can never remember which card to pick up.

You can't believe how shitty your memory is.

> CD: Grab the deuce of clubs.

You pick up two LICORICE GUMMY BEARS.

These need to be stored for safe-keeping as soon as possible. Finding your BACKUP HAT has never been more urgent.

> CD: Pick up all of the cards and throw them at Doze.

The deuce of [whatever suit] is always the card that doubles as the two pieces of candy they store in their hats. Deuce's deuce represents his precious cargo of licorice gummy bears. I don't remember why. I guess because it's cute or something. Clubs and Spades have black candies, while Diamonds and Hearts have red candies. I think of everything and leave nothing to chance. Can you imagine if I actually did something useful with my life to benefit humanity? Wow, me neither. (Sounds bad.)

 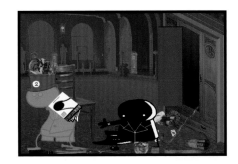 

You pick up a bunch of cards and fling them Doze-ward.

Didn't accomplish a whole lot, other than put some of your
private reading material on embarrassing public display.

> CD: Pick a card, any card.

You're a busy guy so you just pick up any old thing and put it on your head.
Since you are in a big hurry you will assume that it is your BACKUP HAT.

You stand nearby the two remaining cards on the floor. An OFF-SUITED KING AND JACK.

> CD: Pick up card depicting stately blonde-haired fellows.

Each MC member also has their own pornographic magazine of choice. *Black Inches* is literally the name of a real porno magazine but has been invoked here to refer to a great length of black licorice instead of a tremendous penis. It is also the name of Snowman's whip, which simultaneously references the aforementioned pornography and contrasts with Jack's devastating later attack, called Red Miles. There is nothing whatsoever so small, pointless, or maddeningly stupid in this story that it does not in some way fit into an established framework of patterns, systematization, or categorization. To what end, you ask? Oh. I see you didn't. My mistake.

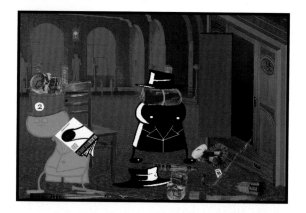

You aren't going to stand around jack king off all day long, so you grab the JACK OF DIAMONDS.

Oh.

Here's your BACKUP HAT. Problem solved, you guess.

> CD: Forget you are CD. Believe you are Hearts Boxcars.

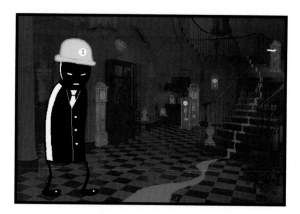

You suddenly remember you are Diamonds Droog.

Whoever took your hat is about to discover he's the unluckiest man on earth. He better hope you find him dead. What you're gonna do to him will be much less painful that way.

> DD: Wear backup hat.

You don't have a BACKUP HAT all you got is this DECK OF CARDS oh wait yes you do.

It's stashed away in your BRAWLSOLEUM.

> DD: Retrieve hat from brawlsoleum.

Readers took advantage of their freedom to submit commands mainly by trying to come up with inventively stupid ways of convincing me to switch the focus to a different character with "Be the other guy" type of commands. I almost never cooperated, because that would've been malpractice. Sometimes I feel like not many people appreciate the fact that "reader-influenced storytelling" never meant the readers actually got what they wanted. It virtually always meant they were given ANYTHING AND EVERYTHING EXCEPT for what they wanted.

You are the only member of this band of thugs who is civilized enough to keep more than one BACKUP HAT, as well as an extensive array of FINELY TAILORED SUITS.

The BRAWLSOLEUM seemed like the best storage option for your exceptional wardrobe. If there's any better sort of compartment to keep your wardrobe in, you'd love to hear it.

Also there's a shitload of guns and cards in there too.

You put on a BACKUP HAT.

> DD: Withdraw licorice fish from backup hat.

Whew. Your SWEDISH FISH are there.

This is why it's a good idea to always store your candy in your BACKUP HAT rather than your usual one. Other members of your gang have learned this the hard way and they're finally starting to catch on.

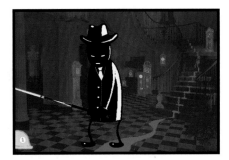

Suddenly you get coldcocked in the face from the future.

You'd know the knuckles belonging to that suckerpunch anywhere.

I'm now so confident in your ability to parse playing cards as items that I saw no need at all to actually depict the Swedish fish. In fact, you barely even noticed he was holding a card, and not fish, until I pointed it out here.

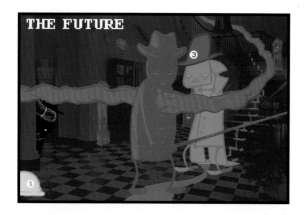

Trace always knows where you've been.

The spineless rat likes to follow your PAST TRAIL around and mess with you.

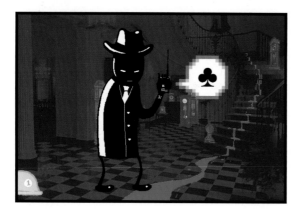

Trouble is, whenever he does, he lets you know exactly where he's going to be in the future. This time you'll be ready for him.

You radio Deuce for backup. Give him a time and place, and exactly what path through the mansion to take.

> DD: Resume pursuit of wounded felt member.

You don't know if the wounded guy went up the stairs, or came down. Or who wounded him, and when. Might have even been you, for all you know.

> DD: Follow trail of blood up the stairs.

Trace follows, *Donnie Darko*-style, past trails people leave invisibly wherever they go. Fin has a similar power but follows future trails. Both Fin and Trace are a little sharky in design. (Fin especially, which is the only way in which his name is loosely tied to his power.) Their powers of detecting and following the subtle trails left behind that no one else can sense is somewhat like a shark's ability to smell tiny traces of blood in the water and track prey for miles. This is why they're kinda sharky guys, why they have those powers, and why they're named those names...or some other jumble of cause and effect I don't remember. It's like the famous question: which came first, the biscuits or the eggs?

288

Can't overthink this time stuff.

You go with your gut and head upstairs.

> CD: Follow Diamonds Droog's instructions.

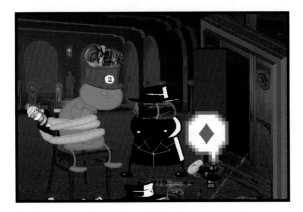

After giving a quick 10-4 over the RADIO, you take another look at your prisoner. He lucked out. Looks like round two of your brutal interrogation will have to wait.

You couldn't find any ROPE, so you tied him up with a STRETCH ARMSTRONG DOLL which you happened to have lying around. You don't remember how you got it.

It looks sort of dumb, but it will have to do.

> CD: Just lock Doze in the battledrobe.

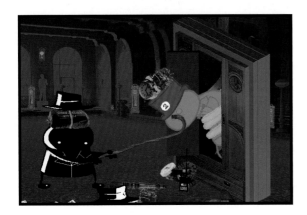

Time to hit the road. You beat your hostage into the back of your BATTLEDROBE with the BULL PENIS CANE.

Wait this is a BULL PENIS CANE?

Gonna be honest here. I don't have the foggiest idea why Clubs Deuce has a Stretch Armstrong doll, or what that's even doing in this comic. One of the extremely rare instances of free association madness that was allowed to seep into this comic while for two seconds I suffered from an almost unheard-of breach in creative discipline and took my "eyes off the prize," as they say.

You flip the fuck out over the fact that
this is apparently a BULL PENIS CANE.

> Meanwhile, running roughly parallel with
present events.

Actually, when I was rummaging around Google for cudgels and canes for Clubs Deuce to keep stockpiled, I don't think I realized that particular one was a bull penis cane until later. Once it dawned on me, CD's BULL PENIS FREAKOUT PANEL was completely autobiographical, much like John's Gushers revelation meltdown.

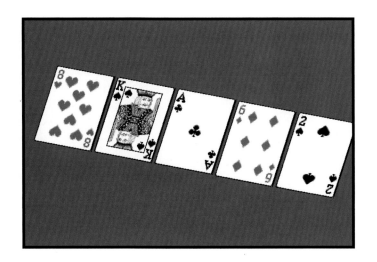

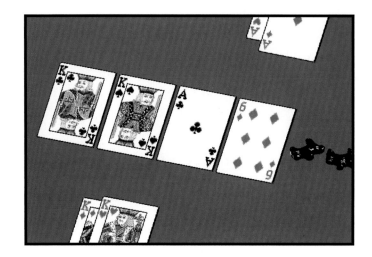

Itchy always cheats. But he's always cheated for the last time.

You're gonna jump to a timeline where he's dead.

Wait, you can't tell what's going in these panels without animation... Itchy very quickly swaps the eight for a king, giving him four of a kind and winning the hand. Also notice the two of spades turns into licorice Scotties. That isn't Itchy cheating, though. That was me cheating the laws of physics.

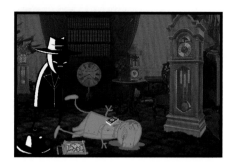  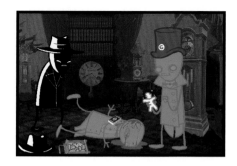

Looks like he got what he deserved.

But, uh...

As usual, you find yourself in a bit of a predicament.

> SS: Make friends with Die.

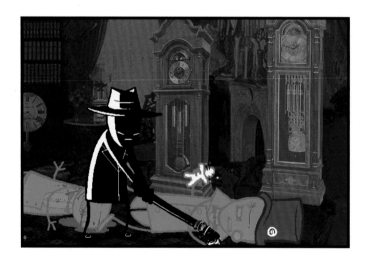 

You introduce your CAST IRON HORSE
HITCHER to your new friend.

Die scrambles for a PIN he's been
saving for a special occasion.

Die is a petty bastard, but ultimately he's a coward. He doesn't favor confrontation so much as exacting his revenge by jumping to a timeline where the guy he's cross with has just been offed by someone else. I'm not sure what gratification he gets from this exactly. Especially since it seems to have a tendency to put him in the exact same danger that the guy he had a beef with just got killed by. Like in this case, a drub-happy horse hitcher.

How many times does he have to tell you. He made this town.

> HB: Stop being SS.

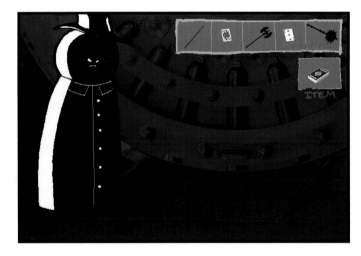

You stop not being Hearts Boxcars.

You have made your way to the Felt's SECRET VAULT.
It's bigger than you were expecting. You doubt you
will be able to rely on your usual safe-cracking
method, which is prying it from the wall with your
bare hands. You'll have to think of something else.

> HB: Do a silly dance.

This is just absolutely the most ridiculous thing
you could possibly choose to do right now.
I mean come on.

Why don't you take a closer look at that safe...

Seriously stop that.

> HB: Pry the wall from the safe.

Die transports to a timeline where Slick was killed long ago. The town was never built. For the first time, we briefly glimpse the alien world this romp is taking place on.
(HINT: IT'S ALTERNIA.)

That notion is even more ridiculous than the last one. Wait who are you kidding no it isn't.

Looks like the combination to the safe is entered via the hands of the clock. And you somehow doubt spinning the hands around manually is going to cut it. Knowing these guys, you've got to alter the flow of time itself to make it work.

Which of course is bullshit. You think you'll just blow it up instead. Time to get Deuce on the radio.

> HB: Deploy PUNCHBOX.

You deploy the WRATHTUB.

> HB: Retrieve two of hearts from backup hat.

You retrieve your pair of WAX LIPS.

If anyone tried to steal your WAX LIPS, you would eat their eyeballs and deliver an angry lecture into their empty sockets.

> HB: Peruse Red Cheeks magazine.

At this point readers were trying to anticipate and/or influence what wacky name I would give HB's storage unit. "Wrathtub" is so much better than "punchbox." Sorry, random guy whose identity is lost to the sands of time and never mattered at all.

Just glancing at it gives you palpitations.

Literature for avid CARDIOFICIONADOS such as your self. Those burgeoning red humps... that miscievous little tail... the snug, welcoming cleft...

The saucy imagery is hard to beat. Harder than what you beat inside your chest now. Your heart is what you're beating.

You beat it to RED CHEEKS MAGAZINE pretty regularly, you'd say.

> HB: Call Clubs on nearest card.

You radio Deuce on the 10-4 cards. Let him know you you need a powdermonkey on the double.

You hear ticking. And it's not coming from the big VAULT CLOCK above.

You hope it's not what you think it is...

Oh no. Oh God.

It's Biscuits. His OVEN TIMER is ticking. This is no good.

Cardioficionados...masturbation jokes...powdermonkey on the double... This page is on fucking fire.

Ugh, there he is.

This idiot thinks his special oven transports him into the future by the amount
he sets on the timer. Well, he's sort of right. But in reality, all that's
happening is that he's hiding in there until the timer's up, then pops out.

You guess he's relatively harmless if he's alone. You can take him.
What you really have to worry about is if he teams up with...

Oh no. That ringing. That godawful ringing. You can hear it...

When I was thinking of Eggs and Biscuits, I thought it would be funny if there was a sci-fi story where people used time travel, but everyone using time travel was aggressively stupid, didn't hesitate to use it for any reason at all, and never, ever stopped using it once they started. Of course, writing such a story would entail creating an insane mess far beyond even *Homestuck*'s standards. This way, I didn't really have to write it. I just had to introduce the characters, check back on them now and then, and document HB's gradual descent into inconsolable despair.

Eggs.

Son of a FUCK.

You might as well just grab one of your
axes and kill yourself now.

> CD: Follow path.

In the future, you've already followed the path
through the mansion that Droog told you to.

Trace followed Droog's PAST TRAIL even further back,
but found a much fresher trail crossing his path.

Looks like this little guy's talking on the radio.
Says something about how he'll be right there once
he gives Droog a hand.

Trace decides he'll trace this guy for a while, see
what he's up to. And then mess with him of course.

Son of a fuck, indeed. Hmm, hang on. I guess Trace can also...hear the past trails talking? I never thought about this feature of his power much, but it really offers a lot of snooping possibilities. If he enters a room and suspects a bunch of people were talking about him, all he has to do is wait for them to leave, then listen to their past trails talk to each other and eavesdrop on their conversation. He's probably busted SO many people in this mansion gossiping about how neurotic and insecure he is.

297

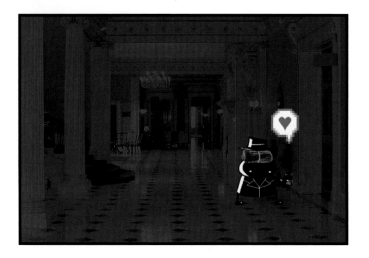

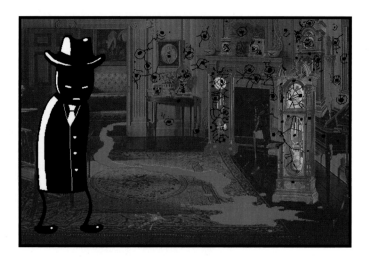

In the present, you talk on the radio.
Say something about how you'll be right
there once you give Droog a hand.

> DD: Take a good look around the new
room you're in.

Looks like the trail of blood ends here.
Or originates. Whatever.

Something went down here in the past. Or... is about
to go down in the future? You know what, never mind.

21/1000 CLOCKS DESTROYED, APPARENTLY

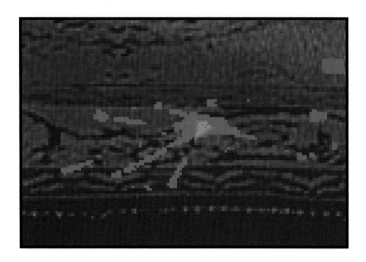

Hang on. There's a tooth on the floor. You know
that tooth. You've felt its bite before.

Fin was here.

And judging by the forensics of the scene, the
angle it hit the floor, the direction of the blood
splatters and how dry the blood is, you think you
know EXACTLY what he's about to pull.

Or more specifically, what he's about to already
have pulled.

The green tooth. The blood. That's some foreshadowing there. Probably the greatest honor you can pay the boss: spitting out one of your own bloody teeth. Anyway.
Fin can see what people are up to in the future, just like Trace can with people in the past. Such as...examining a room he was in, while in the past, looking at the
future trail of the person in that room, who happens to be examining the bloody aftermath of what happened to Fin while he was in that room a while ago. So as you
can see, whatever Fin was doing here in the past, it clearly involved using his power to the greatest possible advantage for himself. He totally didn't get his tooth
knocked out, or get pumped full of lead.

Fin always knows where you're going.

He's followed your FUTURE TRAIL here. He likes to mess with you from the past.

Trouble is he tips you off to where he's been. This time you're ready.

Wait for it. Wait...

 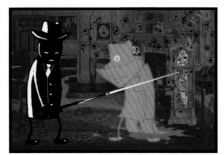 

NOW.

Predestined bullet holes are convenient. Gives you something to aim for.

Good work, Fin. Another time power success story.

7/21 CLOCKS REDESTROYED

> SS: Rematerialize.

That doesn't make any sense.

You never went anywhere.

Die realizes there is a cost to settling the score with you in this way. The cost is having to live in a desert amidst the ruins of a dead civilization for the rest of his life.

He thinks that's stupid, so he pulls your pin.

> SS: Help the green man live up to his name.

Oh, so that's how that blood trail down the stairs we saw earlier got there. This intermission has a lot of fun little points of environmental foreshadowing. But literally all of them are trails of blood, bullet holes, and dead bodies.

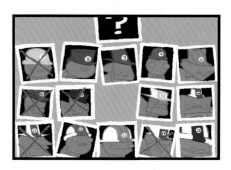

> SS: Take voodoo doll.

You grab his VOODOO DOLL, and stick his pin in there for good measure. Might as well keep track of everyone you've offed this way too.

Not that you intend to abuse its power to settle your score. What's the point if you're not gonna get your hands dirty.

Still, it might come in handy down the road. Lord English is supposedly indestructible. He's rumored to be killable only through a number of glitches and exploits in spacetime. The doll may ultimately help you work the system if it comes to that.

> SS: Clocks. Destroy them.

Spoiler: he eventually does "work the system," in a very Spadesian way. He uses it to revive the entire Felt, take over the gang, and go fight a Lord English stunt double in the form of a different Jack Noir.

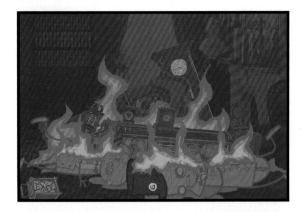

29/1000 CLOCKS DESTROYED

5/15 GREEN TORSOS DEAD

> DD: Follow blood trail downstairs and finish him off.

Problem with that is, he'll just see your FUTURE TRAIL following him, and that'll be nothing but a loud invitation for him to mess with you some more.

Besides, better to leave him alive. You think you know where he'll lead you to. Just got to be a little more subtle about tracing his BLOOD TRAIL. Keep your FUTURE TRAIL out of his line of sight.

> SS: Return to being Hearts Boxcars.

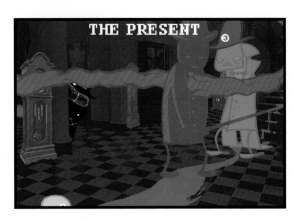

DD's thing is being cool and smart. He's the only one in the gang who's either of those things. Technically SS is smart as well, but his cleverness is frequently undercut by his total lack of cool or discipline. In other words, he is perfect leadership material.

Spades Slick cannot return to being Hearts Boxcars because obviously Diamonds Droog is too busy being Clubs Deuce.

You just watched Trace throw a punch into thin air for some reason. That guy's awfully silly!

He then skulks off somewhere.

You don't realize he's following Droog's PAST TRAIL through the mansion until he gets to the point where it intersects with your trail, at which point he'll start following you.

But we all realized it. Because it's obvious and couldn't possibly be more clear.

> CD: Implement nefarious scheme.

You follow Droog's simple instructions. So simple even a forgetful nincompoop like you can remember.

There's a BLOOD TRAIL on the floor that goes in a different direction than Trace went. You decide to follow it, because that sounds like a really good idea to you.

If there was something you were supposed to do after helping out Droog, you'll be damned if you remember what it was.

Trace catches up to where you were. But you're gone already. All he sees is the long, gross rubbery arm of your PAST TRAIL stretching through the room.

He finds his comrade tied up with the stretchy rubber arms of a small man. But there is nothing gross or unpalatable about that in the least.

Doze unslows himself and begins mumbling something feverishly.

About his hat.

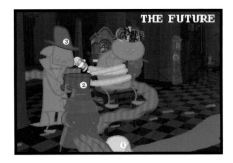

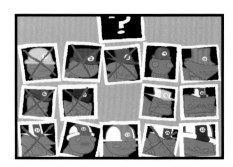

7/15 GREEN TORSOS DEAD

107/1000 CLOCKS DESTROYED

Fin makes his way through the mansion to get some help.

He wonders where this little guy is going. Deuce's FUTURE TRAIL is headed in the same direction he's headed, by sheer coincidence. Fin decides to follow him for a bit, keep an eye on him. For as long as Deuce's path matches his, that is. There's pretty much no chance he's headed to the same place, though. That would be statistically improbable.

He's got no idea what these other goons are up to here. Funny, their FUTURE TRAILS end here. He's not gonna stick around long enough to find out why. He's a bit too woozy from the blood loss to sort out this mess anyway.

> CD: Follow the red-blood road.

The old "hide the bomb under someone's hat" trick. I guess CD earns a kill here? All his kills are earned with bombs. Notably one involving several tons of shaving cream, much later. Oh, I GUESS there was that one time he also murdered a sleeping child using some peanuts.

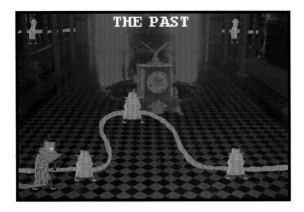

THE PAST

It's uncanny. This little guy is matching Fin's route every step of the way.

HE MUST KNOW SOMETHING.

Fin decides he's got to take him out.

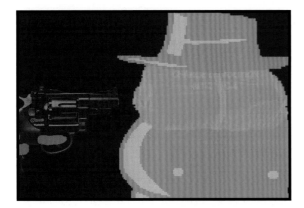

But he can't get a clear shot. Too dizzy, and with all that C4 under Deuce's HAT, firing would be a bad idea.

MY GOD HE'S THOUGHT OF EVERYTHING.

Clearly dealing with a criminal mastermind here.

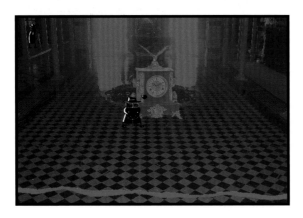

You stop to admire this gorgeous clock. It is so pretty. Too bad it's not ticking like so many of the clocks in this place. Not that you can blame them. There are so many clocks in this mansion it would obviously be impractical to make sure they all work properly.

Oh look. A trail of blood.

You think you'll start following it.

> HB: Waste exactly four hours on this tomfoolery.

Here's a real good paradox. The first true paradox of this criminal caper, possibly. CD follows Fin's blood trail. But at the same time, Fin is following CD's future trail. And in the process, Fin is leaving the very trail of blood that CD will be following in the future. Who is following whom?? It's almost like the one thing that ISN'T being followed, by ANYONE, is the plot. Ha ha :-)

YOU HATE TIME TRAVEL YOU HATE TIME TRAVEL YOU HATE TIME TRAVEL YOU HATE TIME
TRAVEL YOU HATE TIME TRAVEL YOU HATE TIME TRAVEL YOU HATE TIME TRAVEL YOU HATE
TIME TRAVEL YOU HATE TIME TRAVEL YOU HATE TIME TRAVEL YOU HATE TIME TRAVEL

Above, a spectator has appeared at the strike of 4 and has been
giggling at your foolishness for a number of minutes.

Clover would have been tickled to help you open this vault! At the cost
of answering a few of his clever TIME RIDDLES, needless to say.

If only you'd thought to seek his help first, rather than charging like the
silly brute you are into this deadly trap of stable and not so stable time
loops. Mostly unstable, really. These guys are way too dumb to maintain
even elementary looping stability for more than a couple iterations.

If you weren't so preoccupied, Clover could tell you that you could use
Crowbar's help to pry anything out of a time loop, stable or otherwise.

If you weren't so preoccupied, and if he weren't so dead! Hee hee hee!

Eggs and Biscuits creating unstable time loops technically means they're creating tons of doomed timelines. Which makes a lot of sense, since one of the only things the members of the Felt are truly good at is dying.

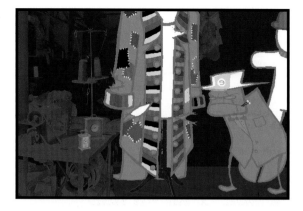

Stitch mutters to himself in his shop. He guesses Eggs and Biscuits are roughhousing again, because the fabric of spacetime is tearing something fierce on Lord English's CAIRO OVERCOAT. This sort of thing is exactly why he keeps a BACKUP COAT, and always leaves Stitch with one of them.

Any gang does well to have an in-house doctor on hand. But if you deal in time travel you better have a damn good tailor too.

> HB: Call Spades for backup.

You tell Slick to get his scrawny ass to the vault. It's goddamn bedlam down here. You tell him you asked Deuce for backup but surprise surprise he's nowhere to be found. Big surprise, you tell him. You tell him that was sarcasm. He says he knows.

Slick says he'll be right there. He'll see if he can round up Droog for support.

Droog says Deuce is tailing Fin, while he is tailing Deuce. He'll be there to help out Boxcars as soon as he and Deuce take care of business with Stitch. Couldn't be simpler.

Oh yeah, he also mentions he pumped Fin full of lead so you can cross him off the list. You roger all that.

The line "any gang does well to have an in-house doctor on hand" seems to imply the Felt isn't all that well constructed, since judging by this intermission, none of its members are actually doctors. Until we meet Doc Scratch, that is. So I guess that makes this line foreshadowing? Oh yeah, I guess it is.

Fin busts into Stitch's workshop blubbering something about watching out for the little guy who's about to come in here. He says to watch out because he's got a bomb on his head which is undoubtedly quite volatile and even the slightest spark would surely set it off.

Stitch sees Fin's obviously in pretty bad shape, and checks his EFFIGY. Sure enough, the thing's in tatters. But he should be just fine if it can be patched up before he bleeds to...

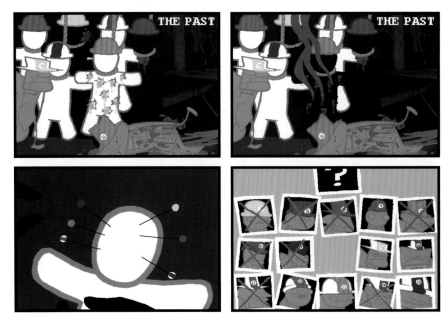

Death.

8/15 GREEN TORSOS DEAD

> CD: Burst in thrusting bull penis cane.

Does Fin die because Slick sticks his pin in the doll? Or by sticking a pin in the doll does Slick just jump to a timeline where Fin just happens to die at that exact moment? Maybe it doesn't matter. Dude got shot a whole bunch of times.

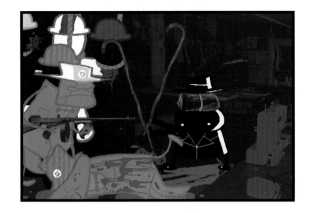

Everybody out of the god damn way. You got a hat full of bomb, a fist full of penis, and a head full of empty.

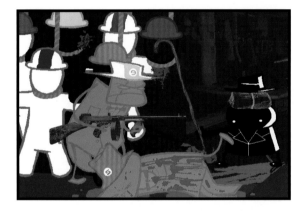

Stitch says drop the livestock knob and settle the hell down.

He says you do realize C4 is a stable explosive and won't detonate with gunfire, right?

You say oh.

> DD: Sneak into Stitch's boutique.

Drop it and get in.

Don't bleed on the suits.

Stitch says huh?

Probably the best line of the intermission (and arguably, all of *Homestuck* even) appears on this page. I don't think I have to tell you which one it is.

You admit the thought of carrying an
imprisoned tailor wherever you go is
gratifying for personal reasons.

But in this case keeping him alive should
be useful in dealing with English later.

> HB: Prod idiots with Red Cheeks.

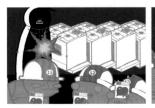  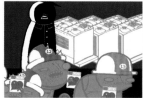  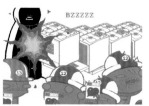

This predictably accomplished nothing!

Taking your smut out of hiding turned out to be a very bad idea. Now copies from the
future are appearing left and right and these clowns have their paws all over it.

SLICK WHERE THE HELL ARE YOU

> SS: Remove Crowbar's pin.

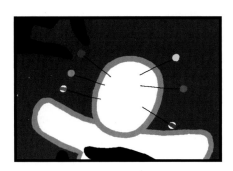  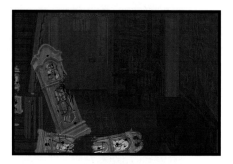

Eggs and Biscuits are digging the hell out of HB's weird, heart-themed porno mags. Can't really blame them. Don't try to pretend like you aren't dying to take a peek inside. Probably lots of shots of somewhat unsettlingly detailed hearts, perspiring slightly like a tomato in a commercial, close-ups fixating on the cleft with some surprisingly artistic compositions...

Crowbar's alive again. And a whole bunch of other stuff is different.

You forgot this gang almost seems halfway competent when he's running the show.

The good news is you get to kill him again.

> SS: Insert and quickly remove Snowman's pin.

You have no idea how much you'd like to. But even you're not that crazy.

Still, kinda tempting.

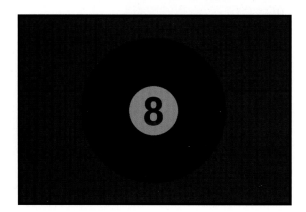

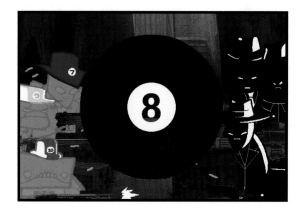

We begin to understand that Crowbar has value to the organization that extends beyond his ability to maintain possession of a crowbar. As the #3 guy, he tends to function as the gang's actual leader, instead of the #2 guy, who has disdain for all of them and uses them as puppets in his grandiose temporal schemes, and the #1 guy, who is never around at all and has barely any involvement with the gang, or with the story for that matter.

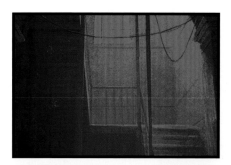

Oh, here's Snowman. (She and Crowbar are definitely hooking up, but you didn't hear that from me.)

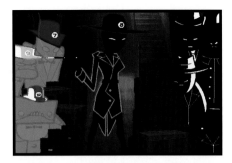

Her text has this spooky fade-in thing going on that you can't see here. She is, for reasons yet unknown at this moment, cosmically bonded with the properties of space. Her life span is linked to the universe itself. One consequence of this, it would seem, is her ability to not be particularly anchored to any concrete location. She can fade to, and fade from, black to scoot around. (This was a longer way of just saying...yo she can teleport.)

313

Spades Slick, who is Jack Noir from another session walking his own path, starts to embody similarities to the Jack we come to know as the villain. Like missing an eye. Whether these are "cosmic coincidences," or Snowman deliberately maiming him to more closely resemble her former employee/blackrom lover, is left as a thought exercise for the reader, depending on how hot the reader thinks that explanation is.

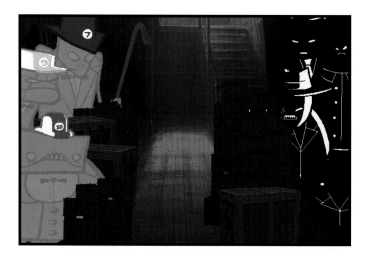

Everyone always ceases gunplay
when Snowman's around.

If you kill her you destroy the universe.

> SS: Remove knife from eye.

It's not a knife. It's Snowman's CIGARETTE HOLDER.

All you know is she's gonna have a hell
of a time getting it back.

> SS: Give it to Sawbuck.

The cigarette holder enjoys object-duality status as well. Sometimes it's a lance, when the story wants it to be a lance. Here, in the panel above, Jack wanted it to be a lance. And the story agreed.

You chuck the LANCE at Sawbuck.

But of course it's only a fleshwound. Seems like that's the only sort of wound you can ever inflict on the corpulent lummox.

Consequently you and he both jump to a random point on the timeline. This looks to be in the recent past, when Stitch and Crowbar were setting up the crates for the imminent gunfight. Which was very thoughtful of them.

Your goons should be showing up any minute with the heavy firepower. For now you've got the drop on everybody.

> SS: Kill something out of rage and frustration.

Stitch gets the business end of your SABER RATTLE. He's dead. In this timeline at least.

> SS: Bring knives to the gunfight.

Where do you think you're going, fatty?

You'll deal with him in a minute.

You whip out your DOUBLE EDGED SWORD and OCCAM'S RAZOR.

> SS: Occam's Razor. Crowbar's head. Make it hapen.

Since the Felt are a time-traveling gang, they often know what's about to happen and when. And seeing as they're a bunch of lugs toiling dutifully on the clock for their boss, they spend a lot of time setting the stage for their imminent gunfights and general buffoonery by moving crates around and setting up props. /shrug/ It's a living.

 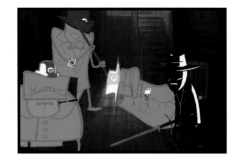 

Crowbar deflects the KING OF SPADES into Sawbuck's unmissable carriage. You jump far into the past.

> Years in the past...

Which is to say the present, for the time being...

A SCURRILOUS STRAGGLER eyes impromptu desert skirmish.

He dismisses them as a bunch of ill-mannered rogues warranting no further investigation. Although he gives a small nod of approval to the plain and serviceable HAT worn by one of the combatants which strikes him as an absolutely smashing display of good fashion sense.

> SS: Hit Crowbar in the head.

You can't kill him yet. You need him alive to return to the original timeline.

You will be taking that CROWBAR though.

> SS: Stuff him in your deck of cards.

This is an awfully tantalizing moment that tells us a lot from a world-building perspective with just a single snapshot. If you're smart, you're just supposed to Get It, put the pieces together, and immediately know what's going on here. Oh, you're not smart, you say? FINE. I'll explain. SS whacks Sawbuck, which sends them all randomly back in time, which reveals they are on a weird alien planet with a pink moon and a green moon. In the distance is an exile, with the initials SS. That's Spades Slick in the distant past! He was in the troll session, got exiled here to postapocalyptic Alternia, wandered the weird desert for ages, then finally "built this town," as in literally took responsibility for the construction of a new civilization, formed a crime gang, started doing crimes in his new civilization, started dressing better, developed a rivalry with some stupid green mobsters, and here we are now.

You cram him in the WAR CHEST.

Sawbuck you need to keep alive too, for the moment. Not to return to the right timeline, but the right time.

Speaking of which, where's tubby think he's waddling off to.

> SS: Just go stab Sawbuck until the time shenanigans stop.

  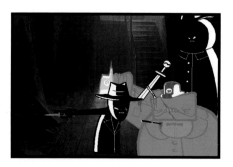

You treat him to a bit of the old BAIT AND SWITCHBLADE.

You appear in the future. You guess this is after the gunfight is over. The gunfight that never took place since you killed/kidnapped everyone who was supposed to be involved. Looks like only Boxcars is here.

> SS: Carry Sawbuck like Titan Atlas would carry the world.

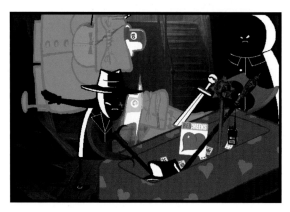

You order Hearts to drop his tub on the double before this fat lard puts you in a wheelchair.

If you take Sawbuck back to your own time and kill him there, that should save you the trouble of hunting him down. Might as well take Stitch too.

Maybe. You're not really sure if that's how it works. You don't really care though.

Aside from sordid dog literature, there are few things that seem to give Slick more pleasure than fat shaming Sawbuck. If there's one thing I'd put at the top of the list to improve morale in the Midnight Crew, it'd have to be placing a much greater emphasis on body positivity.

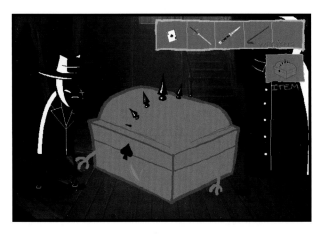

You dump them in the WRATHTUB, then stick the tub in your own DECK OF CARDS.

But you give Boxcars back his sordid literature, which he'd carelessly left in plain sight. No one will ever catch you leaving your smut around. And even if you did, that copy of TERRIER FANCY MAGAZINE could belong to ANYBODY. No one could prove nothin'.

> SS: Stick Crowbar's pin back in again.

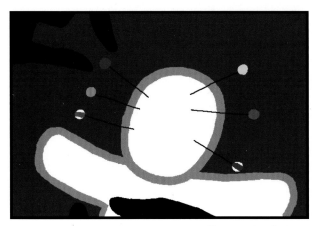

You go back to your original timeline.

But now, stuffed in your chest you've got a live Crowbar from another timeline. Brought to the timeline where he's supposed to be dead... so you guess now he's alive in this timeline which is in part defined by his death? Ok, whatever. You should probably just kill him again anyway.

Also Sawbuck from another timeline is in there too. So you guess now there are two Sawbucks? This is getting kind of dumb.

Slick uses standard mobster logic here. He didn't leave that smut around. And even if he did, it could be ANYBODY'S. You can't prove nothin'. He's gonna beat the rap, ya hear?? He's a LEGITIMATE BUSINESSMAN. As it turns out, mobsters are all basically just petulant little boys.

319

You open the chest releasing them both.
Crowbar doesn't look too pleased.

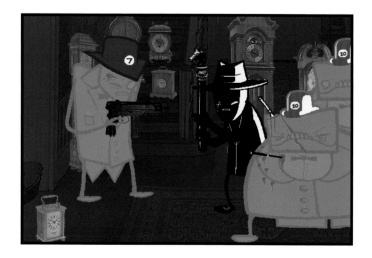

You deflect his gunfire into the awesome gravitational pull of Sawbuck's astonishing girth.

Everybody into the past!

Sawbuck is like the tank of the Felt. He's there to absorb a huge amount of damage for the party. Except the key difference here is that it doesn't help the party at all.

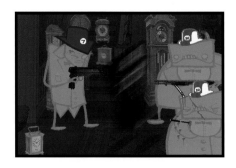  

You dodge his next round too.

It seems Sawbuck from this timeline (i.e. the "real" Sawbuck) was in this
room at this point in time. He and Crowbar exchange bullets. Off they go.

They no doubt go on to spend the rest of their ammunition peppering each other throughout the timeline,
destroying all these clocks in the process between now and the present. You guess that explains the
mess when you got here. Thank God you figured that out. You'd have surely lost sleep over it.

20/107 CLOCKS REDESTROYED. FOR THE FIRST TIME. EVENTUALLY... YOU KNOW WHAT, NEVER MIND.

> SS: Take a moment to think up some time-based one-liners.

Ok you think you got one.

Time travel sure can be a...

DOUBLE EDGED SWORD.

Wait, that was awful. Really really bad. You're sure you can do better than that.

Um, actually? It was fucking great. Leave the commentary to me down here next time.

Let's see... *sorry to*... no... *time's running*... no wait... fuck.

You ask yourself from the past for a little help. *Time's*... something about time. Time being up. No wait, how about some kind of clock pun. No, dammit, will you just listen. You were almost onto something. *Time... time is...*

Screw this. Too many cooks in the kitchen.

Oh and just what does this quivering mound of blubber think he is up to?

> ## SS: Stab first, utter puns later.

Just as you hear your past self asking what happened to your eye, you jab Sawbuck with your BUTTERFLY EFFECT KNIFE. You remember a little while ago asking yourself about your eye, and not giving yourself an answer just before disappearing. Maybe if you stopped and thought about it for a second, you could have warned yourself and avoided the whole mess, albeit in the process of creating a paradox. But your strict policy of stabbing first and answering questions later prevented it. You're sure your past self understands/understood. You are sure of this because you very clearly remember understanding/understooding.

One of the perks of writing sci-fi involving time travel, assuming you are a cool genius like me, is you get to invent new tenses. "Understooding" is an inflection of "to understand," wherein one is currently in the process of understanding something while existing in the past.

You are now Past Spades Slick... again.

You were just about to pull Crowbar's pin. You guess all that stuff with your future self and Sawbuck originally happened in this room while we were all off watching someone else, like Diamonds Droog or something. That makes sense.

> PSS: Remove Crowbar's pin.

Any time you read the phrase "that makes sense" in *Homestuck*, you should be suspicious. But then make sure you crush that feeling, deep down to the place where all your other shameful thoughts go. Then immediately seek the presence of clergy and beg forgiveness.

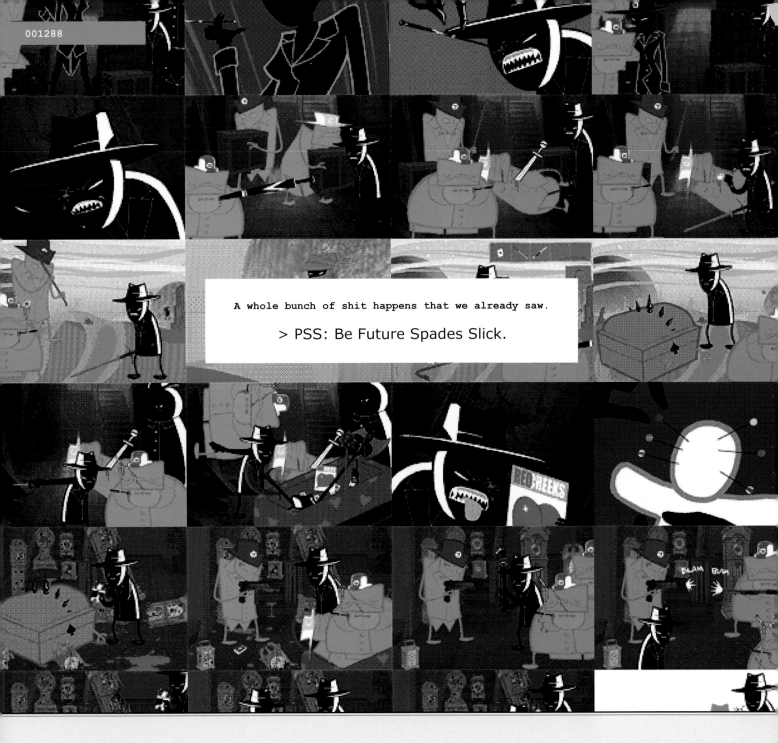

A whole bunch of shit happens that we already saw.

> PSS: Be Future Spades Slick.

Go back to the beginning of the intermission and reread everything if you want to resee all the shit we already saw. Alternatively, if you want to free yourself from this damnable loop of accursed shenanigans, rip this page out of the book.

Being your future self is a lot more constructive because you get to do stuff you haven't already done.

Looks like you're in the future. It's a bloody mess in here. The clocks are more bullet-riddled than ever. And it seems Crowbar and both Sawbucks have been decapitated. You're almost certain this is something you will be, or were already, responsible for. Which of course means more time traveling.

Looks like the tub and chest are gone. Which means future-you must have packed up and left already. Got to take note of these sorts of things so you know where you are in the timeline.

You notice something on the wall over there...

One of the clocks that wasn't destroyed before is now bloodied and full of holes.

Not especially noteworthy. You just have a feeling you should register this fact.

108/1000 CLOCKS DESTROYED

> SS: Quickly remove lance from Sawbuck.

You pry the CIGARETTE HOLDER from his torso. Whoops, another time jump.

This tub of goo keeps going for his gun. Widebody's gotta settle his big ass down.

You really should incapacitate him without inflicting another wound.

> SS: Knock Sawbuck unconscious.

The first sentence here would be quite a wise aphorism if it were actually true. Unfortunately, time makes fools of us all, by giving us an almost inexhaustible future platform for us to continue committing dumbass mistakes we've already made, until one of them finally gets us killed.

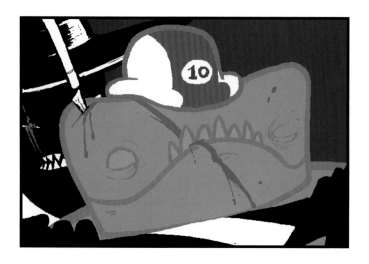

COUNT SOME SHEEP BITCH

Wait... the clock on the wall...

It hasn't been destroyed yet.

But it's about to be. It's ticking down to the time it's stuck on in the future.

Maybe if you time it just right, you can end this whole mess in one fell slice.

Sawbuck: Literally commence counting sheep, like the bitch you are.

You've even got an ice-cold one-liner to dish out when the time comes. You've been working pretty hard on it.

Wait for it... wait for it...

Hate to cut and...

Wait, no. Not yet.

Wait for it...

Hate to... no.

Wait...

Hate to cut and DAMMIT. Not yet.

Hate to cut and run.

...

SHIT.

Hate to...

Hate to...

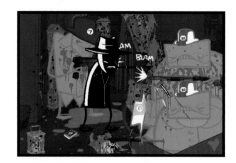

Hate to chop all of your heads off with this sword. Real sorry about that. My bad.

You slay them all with your RAPIER WIT.

9/15 GREEN TORSOS DEAD

2/9 GREEN TORSOS DEADENED TWICE

1/15 GREEN TORSOS DEAD FOR THE FIRST TIME, BUT IT'S AN ALTERNATE UNIVERSE TORSO, SO YOU GUESS MAYBE IT DOESN'T COUNT(?)

7/108 CLOCKS GRATUITOUSLY REDESTROYED

You grab the tub and chest and move on. That is ALTOGETHER ENOUGH of this nonsense.

> DD: Call Spades.

The *Problem Sleuth* one-liner was actually "hate to cut and run." Spades Slick changed it at the last minute to some wiseass shit because he was sick of waiting. Also, "Rapier Wit" is the name of his rapier, which you pretty much have to use while saying one-liners. Because it's witty.

You check up on Slick's status. Slick says he killed Crowbar again, Sawbuck twice, and
Stitch once. You ask him if it was an alternate timeline Stitch. He says he guesses so.
You say that doesn't count. You've got the real one here. He mutters some foul language you
can't quite make out, but you tell him never mind and hurry down to meet you at the vault.

He says he took some damage from Snowman. You say you know. You're having some
EFFIGIES made of yourselves with your BACKUP HATS. Deuce brought Slick's crumpled
BACKUP HAT which he wound up with somehow. Not sure what happened to Deuce's.
Boxcars is obviously tied up at the moment, so you can't get your hands on his yet.

Slick says he's got both their HATS and he'll be down ASAP. You say alright.
He says in the meantime see what you can do about this eye.

> DD: Have Stitch patch up SS's effigy.

Get to work, threadmonkey.

> SS: Have right eye patched up.

Strong appreciation for CD keeping Stitch at bay with the penis cane while DD's on the radio. What a trouper.

DAMMIT.

Your sprite was flipped the wrong way.

You get Diamonds on the radio and tell him to undo it and wait until you're turned around. He says it's the right eye, right? Were you facing left or right? You say it's only right when facing left. It's the left eye when facing right. He says oh, so it's the left-right eye. You say yeah, but hang on a minute, you'll turn around so it's right-left. He says ok, he'll wait.

That's better.

> SS: Arm yourself, in case Cans shows up.

If Cans shows up, none of these weapons you've got are going to do any good.

You admire the LANCE for a moment. It's a pretty sweet weapon with outstanding craftsmanship. At least you got something out of the eye-gouging. She'll have to pry this thing from your rigid severed arm if she wants it back.

> SS: Ride around on horse hitcher pretending to joust.

The MC Intermission is one of the only places in the story where sprite orientation is presented as consequential to the experienced reality of the characters. In the very early days of *Homestuck* sometimes readers would say, "Wait, why is the ghost on John's shirt facing the wrong way?" It's because the sprite is flipped, you clowns. Most people get it though, because most of us play games where sprites flip and details jump from one side to the other, and it's perfectly fine because on some level we all understand it would be stupid and inefficient for artists to make brand-new sprites just to alter directional details to keep characters on model. So this section plays around with that a bit, implying these guys are aware of the bizarre rules of asymmetry in this world, and that the concepts of "left" and "right" are malleable ideas dependent wholly on which direction they're facing. It also assumes a stage-world (i.e. a panel) wherein there are absolute left and right directions. This is a bit weird and counterintuitive to us, because believe it or not, this is not how our own world works.

YEEEEEEEEEEEEEEEEEEEEEEEEEHAAAAAAAAAAAAAAAAAA...

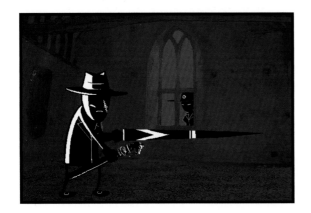

AAAAAAAAAAAAAAAAAAAAAAAWWWWWWWWWWWWWOHSHIT.

  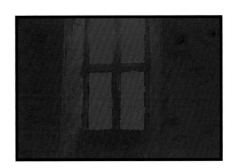

Not to brag or anything, but I think the Snowman fade-out at the bottom there communicates such an INTENSE disdain toward Slick in such a simple way.

You can't BELIEVE she saw you horsing around like that. You will never live this down.

> DD: Shoot up biscuit and eggs's effigies.

Stitch keeps their EFFIGIES in a big warehouse several miles away because of their ridiculous duplication tendencies.

You're sure as hell not going to drive all the way over there, so you just shoot at them in person.

This was such an unbelievably terrible idea.

Note that in any given Eggs and Biscuits mob, there always seem to be a few making an earnest plea for everyone to just chill out and read this dirty magazine.

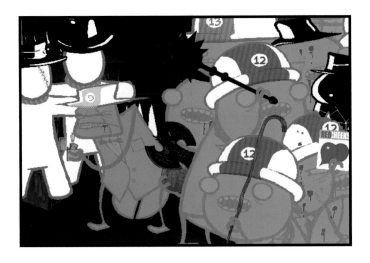

This is incredibly delirious biznasty.

> SS: CHARGE!

> SS: Start whacking things with the crowbar.

I could explain the presence of the green bro there. Really, I COULD. But I'm afraid I'd be tipping my hand re: the true meaning of *Homestuck*. All its mysteries, its riddles, its rich symbolism, laid bare for you in one fell swoop. No. You're not ready.

The first thing you whack is Eggs's EGG TIMER.

You do this because of course you know that Crowbar's CROWBAR will destroy any temporal artifact and completely negate its effect on the timeline.

> HB: Attempt to eat Eggs.

The crowbar is a pretty relevant object. This unassuming maroon tool makes it all the way to the bitter end of the story, smashing this thing and that. Its ability to "destroy a temporal artifact" seems like an arbitrary property for a Felt weapon to have at this point, but it fits more broadly into lore developed much later on. The egg timer is a juju. The crowbar is a juju breaker. Anything that qualifies as a juju, or has juju-like qualities, can be destroyed by this thing, making it an extremely powerful and consequential object that is also a juju itself. By my even saying the word "juju" here, two things are happening. One, the word "juju" now sounds kinda funny. And two, I'm getting ass-deep into cherub lore, which is DEFINITELY something I shouldn't be doing in such an early book.

Your attempt was an overwhelming success.

Biscuits is looking a tad snug in his muffin tray.

He thinks it's about time to poke a broomstraw in this battle. His dough will live to rise another day.

SEE YOU IN THE FUTURE, SUCKERS!!!!!

> SS: Crowbar. Biscuits' oven. Make it hapen.

Just so you know, poking a broomstraw in a cake is a fairly old-fashioned way to tell if the cake is done baking. How did I know this? I'm not even sure. I'm not sure how I know a lot of things I know.

You deal the oven a wicked flogging
but not much happens.

The oven doesn't really have any magical
time properties to be negated. It just
travels into the future at a rate of one
second per second, like everyone else.

> CD: Put dynamite in oven.

You set the bomb to go off in a few
seconds, when both it and Biscuits
are released from it in a few hours.

> CD: Turn up heat on Biscuit's oven.

You're pretty sure this oven doesn't actually work at all.

You just wheel it off somewhere else in the mansion so it can explode in peace.

Here's a nice moment where the full crew is standing together as buddies. They use teamwork and friendship to solve the problem of how to destroy a very stupid man's oven. Let's appreciate it.

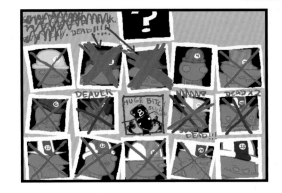

12/15 GREEN TORSOS DEAD

PROBABLY SOME MORE CLOCKS DESTROYED TOO

> SS: Use crowbar to pry the safe open.

Since your expert safe cracker apparently
spent the last five or six hours being
totally useless down here, you figure it's
time to take things into your own hands.

Huh? What's this little fella all worked up about?

Clover insists that you reconsider! Using that
to pry open the vault would be EVER so much
bad luck! Like breaking a thousand mirrors all
at once! The sort of mirrors that tick and
have numbers and tell time and stuff. That is
the worst kind of mirror to break, luckwise.

> SS: Politely ask Clover to remain calm.

Clover dances a lot. It's revealed much later that whenever he dances, in truth he's being a frisky little slut. This is a canon fact.

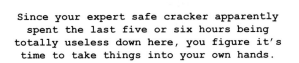

He refuses outright and starts
doing a really frisky jig!

DOO DEE DOO DEE DOO DOO

DOO DEE DOO DEE DOO DOO

He begins spinning a fanciful series
of riddles illuminating the true path
to opening the vault. Mysterious music
fills your ears as your mind assumes
the shape of a pretzel.

DOO DEE DOO DEE DOO DOO

DOO DEE DOO DEE DOO DOO

DOO DOO DOO DEE DOO DOO DOO

DOO DEE DOO DEE DOO DOO

This is how the music would sound if
we were listening to it right now.

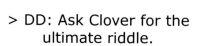

> DD: Ask Clover for the
ultimate riddle.

You ask Clover to open the safe.

This isn't going to work. Clover's too lucky to be threatened by a gun. Don't believe me? Okay, just check out the next page, hot shot. DD is pretty smart, though.
Causing someone to suffer minor inconveniences and humiliations is a pretty good end-run around a supernatural Luck Field. Try to keep this cool tip in mind the next
time you find yourself in a bitter feud with a leprechaun.

What's this? Hee hee! You think you can shoot Clover? He is so lucky the gun will probably jam or something predictable like that. Nice try though!

You just start whacking him with a newspaper instead.

You don't have to be all that unlucky to get whacked around with a newspaper. It's sort of a gray area.

> DD: Check personal ads of periodical.

This isn't a real newspaper. It's just a wrapper for your private sordid literature, which no one can ever see.

Uh oh, it's slipping out a bit. Your appetite for MONOCHROME BEAUTIES is nearly on public display. Gotta keep a lid on that smut! Especially with Clover around.

Here is some of the only legitimately NSFW material in HS. Droog has too much class to get worked up about ridiculous heart pornography, licorice whips, or Scottish terriers. It's fair to speculate as to whether his fixation on gray women has something to do with his exposure to trolls as an Alternian exile. It is also fair to speculate that the "Gray Lady" is an old nickname for the *New York Times*. It's fair speculation because it was a deliberate reference I made, and is, you could say, the joke.

Suddenly the whole vault room is shaking. You wonder what it could be.

It sounds suspiciously like Cans is about to plow through the wall Kool-Aid Man style.
You pray to God that it is not Cans about to plow through the wall Kool-Aid Man style.

All of a sudden Cans plows through
the wall Kool-Aid Man style.

Oh No!

> DD: Resist urge to shout "Oh Yeah!"

You can't believe Cans plowed through the wall Kool-Aid Man style.

S	M	T	W	T	F	S
			1	2	3	4
5	6	7	8	9	10	11
12		14	15	16	17	18
19		21	22	23	24	25
26	27	28	29	30		

He punches you into next week.

You find yourself going about your business a week later. Looks like you're doing a little grocery shopping.

You're a bit confused, having no memory of the previous week. You have no idea what is on your grocery list. Are you out of milk?? What kind of produce do you need to stock up on??? It is all a little overwhelming.

And to make things worse,

the selection has too many
....
PRICES and
VAULES

> HB: Use Eggs' body as bait for Cans.

BATTLE TECHNIQUE

Here's some *Sweet Bro and Hella Jeff* text, which quite probably links to the *SBaHJ* comic that this line is from. Curious to see it?? Well too bad, I'm not printing it here. I think you'll agree we're wasting enough paper as it is. Anyway, this is a very good gag, as well as a good time-travel power for a big, strong man to have. Knocking someone into next week? That's fucking great. Keep this ability in mind for about 6,000 pages later, when Cans's panel-breaking punch power returns as an ongoing excuse for me to continue dazzling you with multimedia fuckery.

You flail the torso Cans-ward in an attempt
to placate him with the red meat.

It doesn't work!!!

Cans clocks Boxcars entirely out of the current calendar year.
You land in a totally different outdated calendar.

TORSO FLAIL is a *Problem Sleuth* attack. Sorry, I have to point out each and every PS reference. I'm obligated to. Also, one time someone at a convention gave me this exact "Spirited Horse" calendar. They modified it with little paper cutouts of Hearts Boxcars in every month's image, exactly as they appear on the next page. I had it for a long time, but alas, I think it was thrown in the trash at some point.

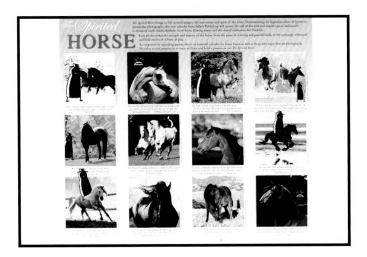

Looks like this one's themed with SPIRITED HORSES. You'll be up to your ass in horses for a whole year. Just great, this is just what you need to be doing. Farmin' all these goddamn horses. Fuckin' pain in the ass.

> SS: Ignore him and just pry the safe open.

You don't care what the consequences are. You're going to crack open this safe and be done with it.

This whole intermission was starting to get a little punchy anyway.

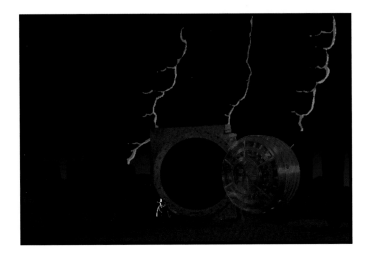

HB is an ungrateful bastard. He died and went to horse heaven, and all he can do is bitch and moan. He deserves to be killed offscreen by whatever the fuck just happened here with Slick's crowbar and the big safe.

The massive release of temporal distortion from the vault transports you to a highly unfavorable timeline. Looks like the entire mansion was leveled, except for the vault and its enclosure. Everyone's dead except for you and you know who.

But at least the safe's open.

1000/1000 CLOCKS DESTROYED

14/15 GREEN TORSOS DEAD

3/4 BLACK SCOFFLAWS OFFED

> SS: Enter the vault.

There's nothing in here except an opening in the floor. There is a door with a keyhole, and you have a feeling you know how to open it.

You only wonder why English's treasure would be locked behind a door with a spade on it.

> SS: Dramatically use the spade key.

Slick finally uncovers the secret location of English's treasure. But like so many treasure hunters before him, he will discover it's nothing like what he imagined. Kind of like a *Wizard of Oz* trope, wherein English's treasure was in him all along and in all the good friends he made along the way. Except instead of that, the real treasure is killing all your friends along the way and treating them as expendable pawns in your petty quest for revenge. Truly an inspiring journey of personal growth and development.

You guess this is what the SPADE KEY was for all this time. You dramatically wield the SPADE KEY in a matter of fact manner.

> SS: Peek inside keyhole.

What KEYHOLE? It was clearly a BARCODE SCANNER all along. Like the kind they sweep groceries over at supermarkets. That reminds you, you should really do some shopping next week.

You're not going to peek inside because the lasers could blind you in one eye. OH WAIT

> SS: Use rules card for blackjack.

This was never a problem because there is clearly a barcode printed on your RULES CARD FOR BLACKJACK.

As well as your arm. But there's nothing wrong with a little redundancy you guess.

> SS: Get on with it.

For a little extra security, the door has a keyhole lock and then a barcode scanner behind that. Just a bit of DOUBLE AUTHENTICATION to make sure the treasure is SUPER safe. Of course the physical key and the barcode card happen to be the exact same object, so the additional security layer is completely useless. Oh, and the barcode is on Slick's arm too. It's almost like this vault was built for him personally to discover and then open, because it's critical to whatever multi-trillion-year scheme English has been cooking up.

Huh?

Oh are you looking for this well come and get it you contemptuous she-witch.

Inevitably it comes to this, a final showdown of sorts between these two before the end of the intermission. But one has to wonder...what is Snowman actually doing here? She works for Doc Scratch and Lord English, who clearly need Slick to get into this vault. Yet she sure seems to be doing everything she can to mess up his barcodes and prevent him from getting in. It's possible she's just being helpful (to me) by setting up the great sprite-flipping gag a few pages later. It's equally possible that she's just fucking with Slick, because she loves to watch him suffer. Snowman is a mysterious figure, and when her motivations are in doubt, "she's just fucking with you" is as good an explanation as any. She and I are alike in this regard, and as such, she is my waifu. (At least until you-know-who comes along.)

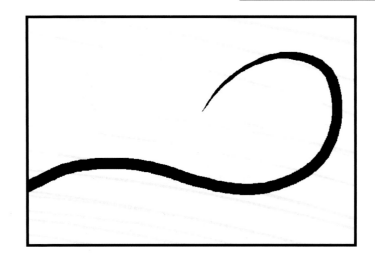

Snowman's **BLACK INCHES** no doubt have been responsible for more than a few **RED CHEEKS**.

It's great that this line implies she's been responsible for whippin' asses raw. Due to the sexual connotations of such behavior. There, I have now explained to you why you are feeling horny, thus completely justifying the purchase of this book. From this moment forward, each author note will actually be MAKING you money.

SLAM

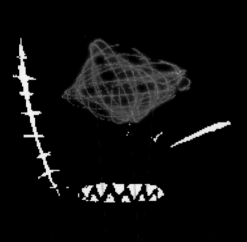

> SS: Flip your sprite.

The scribbling laser pattern on SS's forehead doubles as a stylistic indicator of his anger and frustration. This helps you understand that he is both angry and frustrated. /Puts a big, FAT check mark next to this page number to indicate its author comment has been finished. Reclines in hammock, reaches for lemonade./

you got to
FLIP it.
TURN-WAYS

> SS: Scan the barcode.

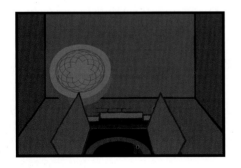

In addition to being a great sprite-flipping gag, this is also a great *Sweet Bro* callback gag. When the gags start layering up like this, that's when you know *Homestuck* is firing on one or more cylinders. Speaking of cylinders, SS just climbed down into a big, secret cylinder. This is his exile station, which has been waiting for him here underground for centuries. The mansion was built up around it as a long-con trap for him to barge through, kill everyone, and end up here so he could start "controlling" Karkat. Who's Karkat, you ask? I thought you'd never ask.

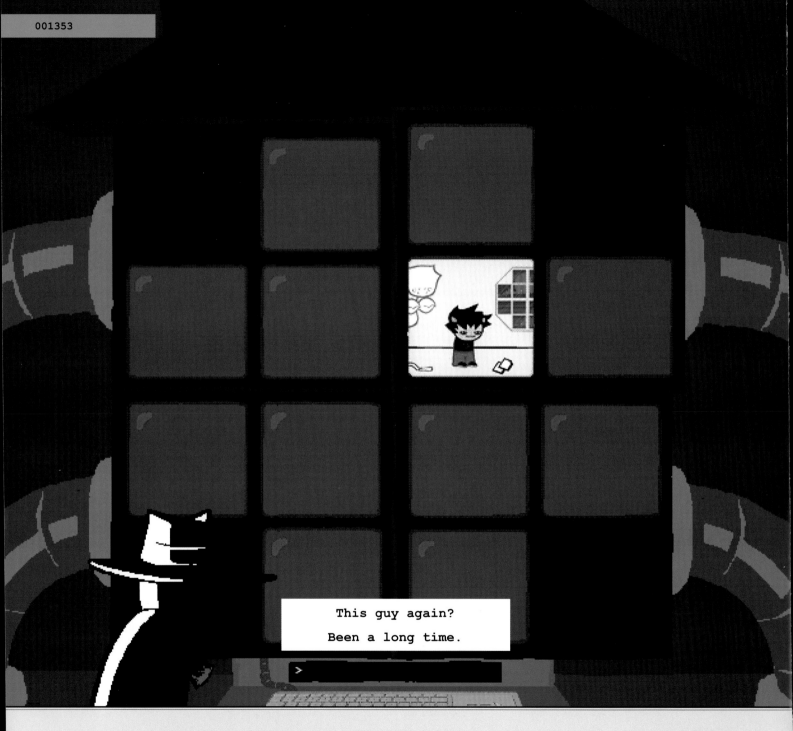

This guy again?

Been a long time.

>

Here's Karkat. See, this intermission wasn't a complete waste of time. Only the overwhelming majority of it was. It does lead back to something that appears to have relevance to the main narrative, and now you are intrigued. It seems that Slick recognizes Karkat, which is also intriguing. What is going on here? Your intriguement is what.

> hey kid_

> yeah you

Spades Slick is to Karkat as the Wandering Vagrant is to John. It's my solemn duty down here in the author notes section to completely and utterly nullify your ability to make inferences on your own. Additional trivia and/or a self-own: why does the button have ==> when the Hivebent "next page" command is ======>? Weird. The lab manufacturers were probably just cheap bastards and only made one kind of keyboard.

This is a cool way to meet Karkat, I suppose, with some fascinating advance tidbits like that crab sprite over there. But—and this is one of the stranger incongruities in the story—his room doesn't actually look like this at all. When Hivebent came around and it was time to actually draw the full environments, I thought this room looked too boring and sterile, so I dressed it up a little more. Ultimately it's not THAT far off, just lighter in tone and missing a recuperacoon (which, to be fair, could have been moved by the server player at this point in his game). In any case, things have many different presentations in HS all the time. Usually characters, but sometimes environments too, I guess. They range from simplistic and abstract to literal and detailed depending on the whims of the artist and the needs of the story. Is there any concrete "truth" behind any presentation? Can any "real" appearance of anything even be said to exist? Somewhere, Plato is weeping. Because he's fucking dead and can't tell me how dumb I'm being.

MSPAINT ADVENTURES

CG: Boggle vacantly at these shenanigans.

It begins to dawn on you that everything you are about to do may prove to have been a collosal waste of time.

>|

> END INTERMISSION.
>

Thanks, Caliborn. You're doing a great job.

353

> END INTERMISSION.

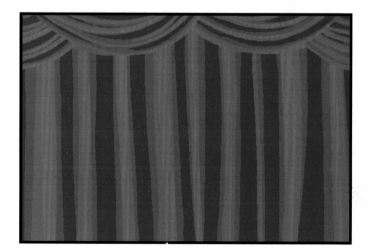

That's a wrap for this intermission, as well as for Book 2. (I think. Assuming this isn't some weird future reprinting I'm not aware of that's the size of three phone books.) Next is Act 4, which is a pretty good act. I don't even remember what happens in it, honestly. I'm looking forward to rereading it, to rediscovering the magic of my remarkable creation. And if you all behave yourselves, I MIGHT just crack a joke or two down here in the bottom margin, a place I like to call the Laugh Gutter. Thanks for reading.

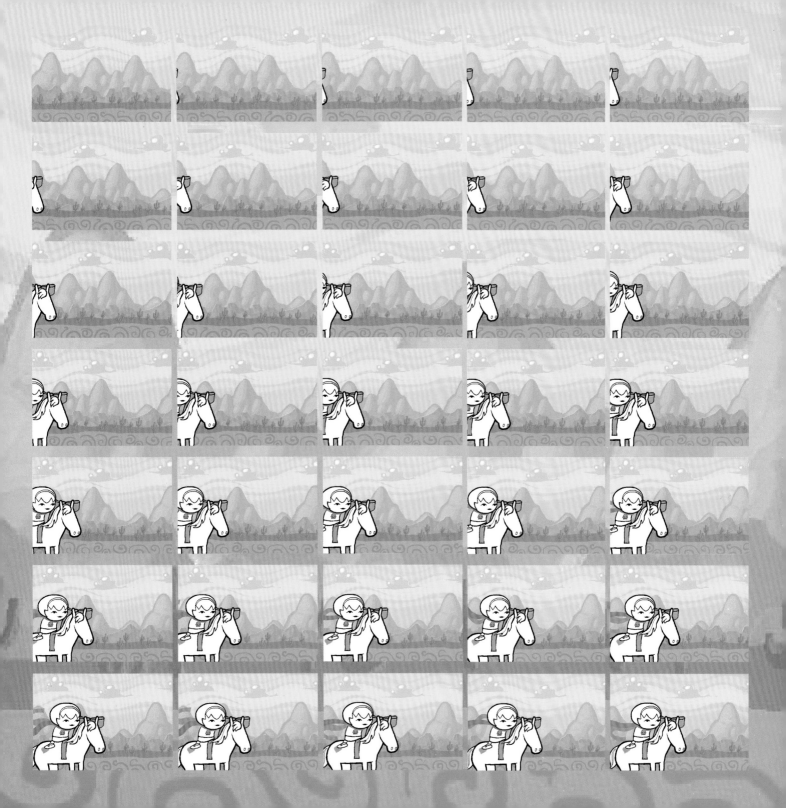

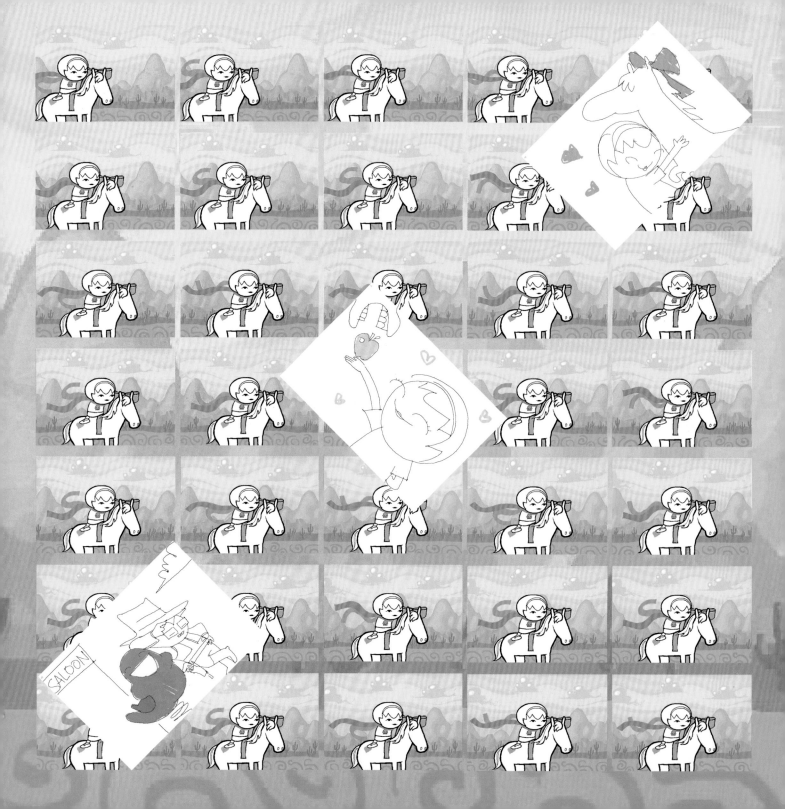

HEIGH

SBURB version 0.0.1

SKAIANET SYSTEMS INCORPORATED. ALL RIGHTS RESERVED.

SBURB client is running.

Homestuck
Book 2
Part 1: Act 3 & Intermission

VIZ Media Edition

By Andrew Hussie

Cover Art — Adrienne Garcia
Book Design — Christopher Kallini
Cover & Graphic Design — Adam Grano
Editor — Leyla Aker

Printed in China

Published by VIZ Media, LLC
P.O. Box 77010
San Francisco, CA 94107

10 9 8 7 6 5 4 3 2 1
First printing, July 2018

viz.com

homestuck.com

PARENTAL ADVISORY
HOMESTUCK is rated T+ for Older Teen and is recommended for ages 16 and up.
This volume contains foul language, Sassacrushin', irradiated foodstuffs, mutant
kittens, grotesque taxidermy, rooftop beatdowns, minion whompage, and Lil Cal.